Becoming the Chef Your Dog Thinks You Are

A NOURISHING GUIDE TO FEEDING YOUR DOG AND YOUR SOUL

Micki & Yogi Voisard, CSD

STRAY DOG PRESS,
CALISTOGA, CALIFORNIA

BECOMING THE CHEF YOUR DOG THINKS YOU ARE
A Nourishing Guide To Feeding Your Dog And Your Soul

Copyright 2001 Micki Voisard

Published by
Stray Dog Press
P.O. Box 1099
Calistoga, CA 94515

Design and layout
HSA Design
4 West 43rd Street
New York, NY 10036

Illustrations
David Voisard
P.O. Box 1099
Calistoga, CA 94515

Book Cover
Robert Howard Graphics

Editing
Val Presten/ Nicola Scott

Library of Congress Catalog Number: 00-193466
ISBN 0-96640-821-7 (pbk.)
Printed in Canada

ℱOREWORD

Micki Voisard and her husband, David, are an institution in our town. Their art embodies and captures joy and life. Micki's unconventional views on all subject matters are taken from her own profound experiences with cancer and her willingness to work with animals that no one will accept. Micki actually likes Shar Peis!

Dietary responsive diseases, especially allergies and intolerances, are well documented in the human and veterinary medical fields. Micki's own experience of feeding unusual foods is testament to the response we expect from dietary manipulation.

Personally, I am a pretty traditional veterinarian with a bent towards "if it won't hurt your dog and may help, you should try it." I am also constantly amazed at the intense response feeding a dog elicits. People do not tell the truth about what they think they feed their dogs and are extremely defensive about what they do feed.

If veterinarians followed the same guidelines for their own feeding, we would be a healthier lot. A few simple, lovingly prepared, balanced meals could not harm your dog, if you follow a few precautions: there are many recipes for well balanced diets (I wish my own was), and don't feed your dog anything you would not eat yourself.

This does not give you permission to feed your poodle half a pound of bakers' chocolate with a glass of cabernet wine, or the latest road kill you have retrieved as "natural dog food." It also does not give permission to feed that bag of chicken skins that are saved from your "low fat, boneless chicken breast" from last week.

Unfortunately, some things do hurt your dog and some we don't know about as yet. Go easy on the herbs and potions designed for people - dogs don't need to overcome the placebo effect and are surprisingly resilient.

It should also be clear, that excellent quality commercial pet foods are just that. Pet food manufacturers don't want to poison your dog with preservatives, and strive to minimize their content and possible effects. A piece of fresh broccoli or a small piece of fresh fish couldn't hurt, unless there are specific dietary responsive diseases that may be affected, including diabetes, pancreatitis, obesity, liver disease, heart disease and so on.

Indeed, a specific home cooked diet can be instrumental in the cure of diseases. My dog eats top quality dog food, cat food, cereal the baby drops. He licks the floor and routinely licks my childrens' faces. The cat food is not by design, but by opportunity, and "Bammer" is a co-conspirator, sneaking the childrens' unwanted vegetables off of the table.

Feed your dog well and love your dog. You will gain joy, and the benefit to you will be immense!

David A. Gold DVM

ACKNOWLEDGMENTS

My thanks to the following people and animals for their help from beginning to end: Antonia Allegra for a kick-start, Adrienne Asher-Gepford for panicked computer calls, Dr. Anthony Gouveia and his wife, Lois, for their special care of my animals throughout two decades and for sharing volumes of information and for being supportive friends, my sisters, Jody Wheaton and Jeanette Stedifor and my dad, Bernie Slingerland, for listening repeatedly about "the book." My dogs, Yogi, for co- authoring, Hannah, for being finicky, my cats, LBJ, Bungi, Opie, Willy, Chubbs and Rocket for leaving my computer alone, my husband, David Voisard, for his fantastic drawings and his willingness to talk about my chapters at 6:30 am, even though he's not a morning person. Veterinarian David Gold for his friendship and fun conversations and his Foreward. And thanks to the many butchers who showed me how to schmooze and gave me extra and the many foster dogs who taught me common sense - (in feeding dogs, anyway!).

TABLE OF CONTENTS

Dedication:

To my mother, Jean, and my good friend, Joan.
Both wonderful women encouraged and supported my "stray dog habit." One day we will all meet at the Big Campfire in the Great Circle of Friends.

In Memory of...
"Dandy," "Dylan," "Sammy," and "Saucy"

INTRODUCTION

"Hey, Barbara - let's eat!"

My name is not Barbara, but I swore the white-haired man was looking right at me. Gesturing for me to come over to his beach house, I headed in his direction, but first looked around to make sure the "real" Barbara wasn't behind me.

I'm a lot like my dogs: I don't normally come when called. But I figured if he thought I was "Barbara," when I got close enough he would recognize his mistake.

"That's it, little lady, c'mon," he chuckled with his arms outstretched.

At this point, I wasn't quite sure if this guy was someone I wanted to meet. A second later, I felt remnants of sand hit my legs and saw a wiry grey streak of something fly by me and jump into the outstretched arms of the older man. That obviously WAS Barbara. I felt a little foolish and pretended to just be walking by his house. The man held up the small dog and said cheerfully, "She sure is cute, isn't she?"

Our conversation about Barbara went on for fifteen minutes, all the while Barbara spun circles around the two of us. She was cute, and she was a happy dog, no doubt. At one point, Barbara stopped her circles and then jumped up and down like a pogo stick.

"She's mighty hungry and she knows I've got something special for her cooked up on the stove." The older man gestured toward the beach house.

"What's cookin'?" I asked playing along.

"Well, let's see...Barbara, what's today? Thursday? It's gotta be FISH STEW!"

With that, Barbara squealed like a pig AND jumped like a pogo stick. She knew what fish stew was and even seemed to know that it was Thursday.

"If it was Sunday, what would you be cooking for Barbara?" I asked, looking into the eyes of the little dog.

"If it was Sunday, Barbara and I would be dining on chicken, of course. We would start with carrots and lettuce for her and mixed greens for me, then move into the main course. Barbara eats her chicken more on the raw side, so the timing has to be just right."

I liked this guy. He had a wonderful imagination and was as playful as his dog.

"Do you cook for Barbara every day?" I asked. "Every day," he said matter-of-factly.

"C'mon in and have a cup of coffee while we watch Barbara eat; she's a riot!"

I sat out on the beautiful deck overlooking the Pacific Ocean just off of Laguna Beach in California. The older man introduced himself as Wade while he brought out coffee for me and a large stainless steel bowl for Barbara. She politely sat staring at the bowl. Wade gestured to her to "go down." Barbara knelt down as in prayer covering her eyes with her paw. Wade called "up" and she sunk her small head into the stew, languishing every morsel and spending several minutes cleaning the bowl thoroughly.

Wade had not been your common-everyday-kind-of-guy. A year earlier, he was immersed in million dollar real estate deals in Los Angeles. At the same time he worked hard to unravel a lifestyle that no longer fit his needs. He didn't know what his needs were until the day Barbara came into his life.

Two years before Wade had picked up his birthday present from his wife at the car dealer. It was a brand new mustard-colored Ferrari sports car. His wife, Glennis, loved the color mustard and thought Wade would also.

Wade was to meet Glennis at a real estate banquet. Not knowing much about his new car or the braking system, Wade drove slower then usual. There was a heavy downpour that evening and he was being cautious.

He was on a side road when his eye caught a tiny figure walking along rapidly, stopping, turning around, looking very confused. Wade could tell it was a small dog. He passed the dog and got a block away when something out of the ordinary made him turn his new sports car around and go back to see if the dog was still in the road. She was. As he turned his headlights toward her she cowered, shivering in the cold downpour.

Before he got out of the car he looked around for his umbrella. "Drats!" he thought. No umbrella, no blanket, or towel to put on the seat for the wet dog. This was his new car, equipped with nothing, not even a flashlight!

Problem number two was that Wade was scheduled to give a speech at the banquet; he was dressed in his tuxedo. It was also his birthday. Glennis was expecting him to make a grand entrance. How would he look when he showed up soaking wet?

A moment went by, and as Wade put it, he "saw his life flash before him." He opened the car door and moved quickly toward the cowering dog still caught in his headlights. He picked the small creature up with one hand and jumped back into the driver's seat. The little dog clung to the lapel of Wade's tuxedo; she was not going to let him go.

"Well, you can guess what happened after I arrived at the banquet. I was a mess, my car was a mess, the dog was a mess and after Glennis saw us, she was a mess!" Wade laughed, just about falling out of his deck chair.

"That Glennis, she hated that little dog. During our divorce proceedings she convinced the judge that I was involved with another woman. She was right! It was that little woman right there." Wade pointed at Barbara, who loved the attention.

"A year ago, I came home and told Glennis that I wanted to move to the beach, give up our other three houses, sell the business, and get rid of that ugly colored Ferrari! She thought I had gone over the deep end and even tried to have me committed. She was almost successful except for a judge who understood that my life was what was killing me. He asked me what I planned to do after I sold everything and Glennis took half of the property. I told him that all I wanted to do was to cook for my dog Barbara and hang out on the beach! The judge said, 'I understand' and he dismissed my insanity hearing."

Barbara was now sound asleep in Wade's lap. He was a man who appeared at peace with his life, but I had to ask him, "Has it worked out like you thought it would?"

"Even better!" Wade said without hesitating.

"Have you ever thought that you might not be feeding Barbara the proper nutrients that she needs?" I asked.

"Hell no, Barbara would tell me if she needs something, we're close." Wade stood up and while stretching, said he and Barbara had some serious beachcombing to do.

Before I left, Wade showed me a picture of him and his ex-wife, Glennis, in the infamous mustard-colored Ferrari.

"Does this look like a happy man to you?" Wade asked, shoving the picture in my face.

He was right, the photo of Wade looked very different. Seeing him that day on the beach would make a believer of anyone. Both Wade and Barbara were being **nourished.** He was feeding Barbara **and** his soul.

I love the word **nourish***. It's not used as frequently as I remember it growing up. It's a wonderful word and I plan to use it a lot in this book.

You can't buy nourishment for you and your dog, it happens. It happens by paying attention, by being aware, by slowing down and listening to the real "hunger"pangs in the lives of us and our dogs. We need to not only nourish the body, but the soul, the mind, the heart, and the environment. How better then to do that WITH your dog. You notice I said WITH not FOR.

For our physical health, we nourish ourselves with food from our or someone elses' garden or from McDonalds. With our dog, we let someone like Purina nourish him, or we supply the nourishment on a daily basis. The WITH part comes into play when after a week or two of "home cooking" for your dog you wake up in the middle of the night and find out you have received as much nourishment from this experience as your dog has. You find yourself actually IN your kitchen USING those pots and knives and food blender that you walked by every day. You find yourself whistling in the kitchen, your dog sitting next to you salivating, getting his stomach prepared for his big feast.

It happened to me.

My kitchen used to be a room to just walk through. Since I was a longstanding vegetarian, meat of any kind, raw or cooked, or for myself or my dog was forbidden. When lack of nourishment showed up in my life, it was time to reassess my worn out path. It was time for a change!

Eight years ago, my physical health was threatened. I had stage 3B metastasis ovarian cancer. The only option for treatment I was given was to do at least one year of chemotherapy.

---

*Webster's definition of the word to **NOURISH**. 1. to feed and cause to grow; to supply with matter necessary to life and growth. 2. to support. 3. to supply the means of support and increase to; to encourage; as, to nourish rebellion. 4. to cherish; to comfort. 5. to educate; to instruct.

I could not buy the idea that there was only one way to treat my cancer. I didn't care who was telling me that or how many degrees he had. I felt that it wasn't possible to be born in this world and not have several options for a problem. I was aware of how many other people died before me of this same disease; I still believed the one choice I was given wasn't the **only** choice.

I ended up in San Diego, California, doing an intensive form of alternative medicine at the Livingston Medical Center, where my immune system was treated, not the cancer. It made sense to me and eight years later, it still makes sense.

During my short recovery time, the familiar path I had been walking had now been torn apart and a new pathway had formed. My three dogs, Otis, Dandy, and Hannah, who had been so loyal to me during my recovery, each came down with cancer the following year. Otis and Dandy were Shar-Peis, Hannah, a Lhasa Apso. My husband, David, and I could not believe it. But why not? If I think about it now, nourishment, or the lack of it, happens WITH whomever we share our lives.

It's contagious.

The new pathway I saw in front of me was a lot like the one Wade saw when he first found his dog, Barbara. Once you see the new path, you can't turn back.

That new pathway is seldom easy, it's usually downright scary. The unfamiliar is something most of us try very hard to avoid. When my dogs got sick, I knew it was more than the fact that they had cancer. Like myself, it became an opportunity to make a change, to see what was on the other side of the hill of commercial dog food. To slow down and "to get **nourished** ."

I dusted off my few pots, found a place on the counter for my food blender and got armloads of books on home cooking for my dogs. It was great and I enjoyed it. Excited about my new discovery I went out in my world to tell pet-related friends about all I was learning and how terrific my dogs were doing on their new food program.

Instead of mutual enthusiasm, I was met with fear and hostility. There was something very familiar to the way people reacted. It was the same reaction I received when they found out I had done alternative medicine to heal from cancer, instead of following the conventional path. Bringing up the idea (that I considered commercial dog food to be one of the main reasons why dogs are getting the same diseases as humans) created panic in the most stable of individuals.

Rational people, who I had thought would jump at any opportunity to do another good thing for their dog, looked at me like I was part of a conspiracy to overthrow the government.

There were people who said: "You don't have a degree in canine nutrition, you're going to kill your dogs" or "You can't do that, it's illegal!" and "I don't see why you would want to do that since the pet food companies have it already figured out."

Having been through a similar scenario with my cancer, I felt the professionals and the lay people doth protest too much! My dogs were dying. I never felt I would accelerate their demise by giving them REAL food.

I continued to feed my dogs their new diet and they continued to improve. Otis still showed signs of advanced melanoma but he lived a normal life, pain free for two more years. Dandy lived four more years and little Hannah is alive and kicking at this writing.

If I look back through my life I can recognize other periods of time when I had moments of inspiration about the care and feeding of dogs. One period stands out the most.

At twenty-one years old I had a job as a flight attendant for an airline that held government contracts to fly troops in and out of Vietnam during the war.

One day my crew and I caught a "ferry" flight from Yokota, Japan, into Bien Hua, Vietnam. We picked up troops in Bien Hua, on a military C-130.

When we boarded the aircraft I heard the distinct sound of barking dogs. The barking got more intense as the nine crew members took our seats. These dogs were patrol dogs, mostly German Shepherds, that were going to Vietnam to meet their handlers and would soon be walking point with a unit.

Two of the handlers were on board. When we reached our altitude, a conversation was in full force, on how the dogs were trained to what kind of food they were fed.

Regular dog food could not withstand the humidity of Vietnam; dry food went rancid in a few days. The dogs were trained to eat C-rations. As the conversation went on, the handlers told stories of how most of the time, after the dogs had been with their handlers for awhile, the food was changed. Despite military orders specifically stating that the dogs were to only eat the C-rations, the handlers shared their food with their dogs. On occasion, the handlers caught a free-roaming chicken and fed it to their dogs. Even snake meat became a part of their diet.

I remember asking a very stupid question. "Why is that so important that your dog eats so well?" (Hey, give me a break I was twenty-one years old!)

If looks could kill, I was dead meat. I heard a growl and I don't believe it came from the dogs.

"Listen, these dogs sacrifice their lives for us. They walk point. Do you know what that means? It means they are the first to survey an area we suspect might be loaded with mine fields; it means the Viet Cong will want to take them out as their first target; it means they do this unconditionally. Do you have any person in your life who would do that for you? These dogs deserve to eat what will make them more alert and keep them healthy. We're a long ways from a veterinarian."

The dog handler seemed to know that he was talking to a very young and naive person, and he ended with a smile and a wink and said, "That's why it's so important."

The young dog handler was not much older than I was but he knew about survival and he knew a lot about dogs. That five hour flight to Vietnam was the most fascinating five hours I have ever spent. Since that experience I have replayed the lecture over in my mind.

Most of us will never be using our dogs like the handlers did in Vietnam. They will be our pets, our guardians, our pals. However, we may feel we share the same feeling as the dog handler - the same intensity, the same compassion.

You have many options about what to feed your dog. You may choose to find a better commercial dog food than the one you are feeding your dog right now. Or you may supplement his diet with home cooked or raw food. Or, who knows, you may become a purist and jump in with all fours and cook entirely for your dog. That decision does not have to be made right now. Give yourself and your dog some time to see what works for the two of you.

Finding books on what to feed my dogs was not difficult. Understanding them was. I got a lot of good information but always felt the books fell short in some way. I resorted to doing the two things I enjoy most when investigating something new - researching and talking to people who were already doing it.

I fashioned my life like a border collie and rounded up a few mentors. They were easy to find, and when I ran out of recommendations, I put ads in several newspapers and flushed them out from there. Everyone I talked with had all read the same books, then went out and created what worked for their dogs and for them.

The missing link in just about everyone's story was what I call the **mechanics** of home cooking. I give my definition of "mechanics" in the first chapter. To me, the mechanics were a staple you could not find at the grocery store and rarely was it discussed in the books I read on home cooking for dogs. **This is a book on the mechanics of home cooking for your dog.**

Once I learned these mechanics, my life became easier. Besides being a good thing for my dogs, it turned out to be a great experience for me. From my first attempts at home cooking, over eight years ago, to the present, I have changed food often and have simplified my life.

The change has come mainly because I have a different dog now

MECHANICS FOR HOME COOKIN'

from when I started. That dog is my co-author, Yogi. Yogi's needs are more complex in some ways and less in other ways than my previous dogs.

Yogi was saved from execution by my friend, Mollie. She saw a good match with the two of us and called me a few days before Yogi was to meet his Maker. I've worked many years with Shar Pei rescue and this ten month old beauty was a prize. His biggest problem was being labeled as "hyperactive," and that he was. I knew I could calm down some of his behavior with food and herbs, but another half of it was coming from a hidden source not yet revealed to anyone. After a few months of living with the most high-strung Shar Pei I have ever spent time with, the truth of his hyperactivity came out while driving in our car. Yogi had a seizure.

I had seen several peculiar movements that Yogi did from the first day I got him from the animal shelter. This time they were all put together and played out in a symphony of pacing, grazing, lip-licking, head jerking, sweating and severe heart beats. Yogi had several seizures within a few days, and he was put on the usual drug of phenolbarbital.

Yogi's food was home cooked from the day he came to live with us. With the discovery of seizures, his diet changed slightly and was stretched out throughout the day. He also was switched over from phenolbarbital to a homeopathic remedy given to him by a holistic vet.

Yogi and I worked together on what food would work for his body and his metabolism. To this day, Yogi will tell me if he's having "one of those days," he'll chase my cats. If it's a real bad day, he'll chase one cat in particular. On his good days, he leaves them alone. With that information we use food that will help him calm down - turkey and butter with honey. Yogi takes his "medicine" with gusto, seeming to know that this will help him. Soon after he savors his snacks, he's back to his normal self.

Just as we need dogs, they need us. Yogi needed someone to understand his needs. When he's in one of his bad-day modes, I've learned how to catch his quick and subtle eye movements. That's not easy with a Shar Pei since their eyes are slanted and almost closed from their wrinkles. The whites of Yogi's eyes are what I look for and when he's chasing cats I see them. Yogi is "telling" me a lot. He needs me to understand his signals.

We have to be careful when we think of the origins of dogs and wolves. A very long time ago, the domesticated dog took a new path to walk - with humans. The author of *In the Company of Wolves*, Peter Steinhart, wrote "that wolves are more serious than dogs. They give you the feeling that they have a sense of purpose. They walk unwavering down a path, where a dog will flit off to the side or become easily distracted. A wolf, to survive, needs to know many things. **Dogs just need to know us.** The wolf has a relationship to the landscape that is far more profound than anything seen in a dog. For a dog, *we* are their landscape. What they need, they get from us. The wolf must be studious and stay focused. Where the dog learns, obeys, and copies, a wolf has insight. A wolf is attuned to all kinds of signals - to the song of birds and the subtle scents of plant and animal drifting on the wind - and these signals tell the wolf where to look for prey or competing predators."

Author Steinhart quotes a conversation with Dr. Harry Frank, a professor of psychology at Michigan State University, and a wolf expert, "It's much more advantageous for the dog to develop a very keen understanding of human behavior and to communicate wishes to a human, because the human is the most important feature of the environment, and we give a lot of visual and auditory cues."

Peter Steinhart injects, "Evolution hasn't honed the dog's problem-solving skills, just its people-reading skills."

If you take the time to make an effort to "listen" to your dog, he'll take the time to "talk" with you. He'll also learn how to read what you're saying and what you're asking him.

In home cooking, it's most important to learn to **trust** yourself and your dog more then others. I admit, it's very difficult to do that with all the "experts" we pay each day to tell us what to do.

Yogi is an expert on Yogi. I can consult with vets and nutritionists about him but he has the final word. He's chosen to chase our cats when he's having an off day. The cats don't seem to mind. They end up on the blanket with him later on when he's calmed down.

Before Yogi came into my life, I spent countless hours listening to hundreds of dogs who "complained" about their food. The SADD (Standard American Dog Diet) program that these dogs were eating was killing them. Fortunately, their human companions got the word in time and changed their diet.

For some dogs, eating a SADD is fine. But for most dogs, it can shorten their life. A lot of breed dogs cannot go for too many years before disease starts showing up in one form or another. Food allergens, severe dermatitis, lameness and a host of other symptoms are just the tip of the iceberg to what could be coming down the road for them. Even hyperactivity needs to be looked at as a serious symptom of nutritional deficiency.

In the chapter on BECOMING A POOP DETECTIVE, you'll learn why it's so important to be a "poop detective." Not exactly your career choice? Too bad. Just like ours, your dog's poop can tell you volumes about him. Reading your dog's poop is necessary in home cooking and is a fun pastime. Your friends will be impressed!

I've taught many people to cook for their dogs, to check their dog's poop, to listen to what they need nutritionally. The biggest hurdle people have is overcoming their fear, the fear of reprisal from their vet, their friends and family, other dog owners. It's learning to hush the "gestapo-within."

This is a good time in our history to break free of old patterns. For over forty some years, we built a belief system concerning dog food, to trust that someone outside ourselves knows best how to feed our dogs. We've done the same with human food. We've trusted that fast food is not only convenient but gives us the vital nutrition that we need. The overweight and disease prone American is the end result. Our dogs are the same, SADD is the canine version of fast food.

I'm going to make an assumption (that's a no-no in the world of writing. A writer should never assume that the reader knows what you're talking about without further explanation). I'm going to assume that you already know that your dog needs a better diet. No matter what your level of experience as a companion to your dog, I'm going to assume that you have already made the decision to do some form of home cooking for your dog.

I'm also going to assume that you and your dog are close. You're buds. Learning to become a better chef for and with your dog is something you've thought about for a while but were afraid to ask. Who would you ask? Many vets don't consider you smart enough to know what is nutritionally sound for your dog. Look at you. They don't think you can figure out what's nutritionally sound for yourself!

I'm assuming you do know. If you don't have a degree in canine nutrition from Cornell University, then you do know it from having many dogs, or reading many books about dogs and/or nutrition, or talking with your dog. That's enough for me to believe in you and your good sense. You've made it this far in life and you can read! Hey, you're more than halfway there!

I used to have a radio talk show called Alive and Kicking. It started out as a show about alternative human health and gradually moved into a show about alternative health for humans **and** pets. It's a natural road to walk when people talk about their health, soon they're also talking about their pets health. People felt very brave telling stories of how their pets were healed from many diseases with **real food.** They came "out of the closest" and confessed over 50,000 watts, that they had been home cooking for their pets for years while lying to their veterinarians.

I love the mavericks, those people who break away from the pack and find their own way. The people who understand that they were born with the ability to look into their heart and mind, to find the true answer and not worry about what someone else thinks, or cower in the corner because someone with a degree or two on his wall suggests that he is the one who can tell you best about your own self, or that of your dog. I am continually inspired by the people I meet who "boot themselves up," who light their own fire, who are worthy of their dog's admiration!

Someone like you! You who are **becoming the person your dog thinks you are!!**

Unedited letters from the Alive and Kicking radio talk show:

Dear Micki,

My mom and me and my dog, Elmo really like your radio show. My dad does to. I mostly like when you talk about dogs. My dog Elmo is my good friend besides my mom and my dad and my computer. I find lots of stuff about dogs like Elmo on the computer and I learn about him more that way. He does not seem to need a computer to learn about me, he was born that way.

I have known Elmo since I was born, he was already here. We have groan together and that is fun.

My mom likes your radio show because she feels she is not alone with what she thinks. She has been cooking for Elmo for his whole life but never tells people. Especially the vet. She says he wont understand but he has a family to and we need to pay him to tell us things we already no.

I will listen to your show more.

Mark F. (age 8) and Elmo
Tucson, AZ

Dear Micki,

I heard your radio show on cooking for your pets and want to tell you that I have been doing that for years. I'm as old as the hills of Arizona and my dogs are too but few people could tell. I share all of my food with my dogs and they have no physical problems.

Some people act real crazy when I tell them about my dogs diet and others seem to want to make a big deal about what and how much raw food our dogs should eat. I call it COMMON SENSE and the longer I hang around my dogs the more gifted they seem to be with common sense then those of us in the human persuasion.

I'll look forward to more of your shows.

Angie Becker (age 83)

Micki,

My dog and I listen to your radio show (he snores, I listen). I like your ideas about health for humans AND animals.

Four years ago I had testicular cancer and my family (wife and 2 teenagers) were very supportive, but it was my dog Marigold who was with me day in and day out while the rest of the family had to fulfill their daily obligations leaving me and Marigold at home to heal.

Everyday we shared food and love, walks and pain, and everyday I know I was becoming more of the person Marigold must think I am. I am back at work but Marigold comes with me, we are inseparable.

Thanks for your show, we enjoy it!
Chandler

Dear Micki,

My mom and me and Elmo cried during your last radio show when you talked about your dog named otis dying. It was so sad. I asked my dad if Elmo would dye and where he would dye to. He said Elmo would go to the planit Pluto. I am going to look up pluto on my computer and read about it. I no it is very far away. Can you describe your dog named otis to me and I will tell Elmo so when he does go there he will be able to find otis and they can eat the same food together. The planit pluto must be the neatest place to go to where there are nothing but lots of dogs. I would like to go there someday. Maybe Elmo and otis can open up a restaurant and serve what dogs eat.

I no you are sad but otis is happy eating in pluto.
Mark F and Elmo

CHAPTER ONE

Quit Chasing Your Tail!

One day I woke up and said, "Stop chasing your tail." I wasn't talking to my dogs, I was talking to myself. I had been agonizing over what or how to feed my dogs and not spend so many hours doing prep work, or research, or shopping. I didn't like to do any of that stuff, I'm an artist. I don't produce, I create!

Reading several dog home cooking books gave me a good start, but I was confused and disoriented. There were just too many "rules." By the time I finished a nutrition book for dogs I felt like it must have been underwritten by a large commercial dog food company. It seemed like a ploy to get me so confused and frustrated that I would give up and go back to buying commercial dog food.

The day I decided to "stop chasing my tail" was the day my dog

Tonto came running in the house with a big smile on his face. He coveted a bone he found buried in the yard. His Shar Pei wrinkles housed the dirt that had come with his prize. This was a great find, considering how popular Tonto was for that moment with my other two dogs. They had "jealous" written all over their body language.

Tonto showed his bone to me but growled a warning to his brothers. I inspected the bone which had been recently buried. Large chunks of dry meat were still present. He took his prize out to the back deck where he devoured it in less than an hour.

The next day, Tonto ate less of his food. He was acting fine, he just wasn't hungry. He wandered over to where he dug up his previous day's cache looking for more prizes. Tonto was a bone kind of guy. When I first got him from the animal shelter, I could tell he cherished and relished bones. He walked around the yard with a bone in his mouth for an hour or so, displaying it proudly to anyone who would pay attention. Then he would consume it voraciously. The other two dogs, also rescued Shar Peis, liked the idea of bones, not the consumption.

There it was, a simple solution to my dog diet frenzy! I watched all three dogs for several weeks, scribbling notes to myself about their behavior and what happened when they ate this or that.

Tonto received lots of bones and fared well with them. He was more of the meat and potatoes type and also loved fruit. He told me all of this by watching him. It also helped to know that he and the other two had ancestry from Asia, being they were Chinese Shar Peis. That gave me more clues as to what their ancestors might have eaten, and thus, what their dietary needs might be.

Otis enjoyed spending his day sitting on his rug outside. Because of an injury to his front legs during birth, Otis was less active. As big as he was, food was not his prime interest. He was into comfort. He savored his food and ate slowly. His favorite food was rice and bananas. He ate meat and veggies and rice. Bananas were his nighttime snack. Because of his "meat mouth" face, it was difficult for him to chew bones successfully. That did not keep Otis from torturing Tonto by hiding bones in his mouth, while Tonto scurried around trying to find his lost prize.

One-eyed Teddi, the most active Shar Pei, loved tennis balls first, food second. He preferred poultry and peas with rice. Bananas were great fun and food.

There is a point to my telling you about my three Shar Peis' diet. **That's all there is to it!**

IS THAT ALL THERE IS?

Yep, that's it. Keeping in mind the definition of **nourishment** and using that as your frame of reference will reduce the chatter in your head about the what if's.

The people I've met who are the most successful with home cooking for their dogs follow this simple truth. Rarely will you hear this from your veterinarian. Most of them feel that a large percent of their clients are not smart enough to figure out what is nutritionally good for their dogs. They are probably right, **but not you!** In the Introduction I discussed the profile of the person who is "born to cook for their dog." You're still reading this book, you must be one of those people!

This book is about the **mechanics** of home cooking. Once you've mastered the mechanics then you're ready to take on the "nutrition experts." If you're serious about **nourishing** your dog, that involves more then just food. You don't have to be as radical as the story of Wade and his dog Barbara in the INTRODUCTION. You do need the desire to make a change and the courage to listen to your intuition.

It takes months, sometimes years to see a health deficiency in a dog. We see it today with dogs fed entirely on commercial dog food. Right now, age seven in a dog is a telltale time in their lives. For breeds like Shar Peis, it is earlier than that, sometimes as early as two years old! Disease sets in in some form or another, or the dog suffers from joint pain or rotten teeth and gum problems.

My recommendation for your home cooking adventure is to start out slowly. That's hard for a lot of us to do. That's where most home cooking diets go wrong. Our "all or nothing" attitude may work someplace else but not with a diet for our pets.

Yes, we have to learn about nutrition, but not from a book or our vet or the lady with five collies next door. These are all good resources, but no one knows your dogs better than you. If we love our dogs as much as we tell everyone we do, then we will trust that relationship and learn from them and their behavior, what we need to know.

The most successful people at home cooking have said they either got their information from being a dog in their past life, or more commonly, they trusted their way through. Trust, that's an interesting word. We expect it **from** our dogs but we live it infrequently. No wonder many dogs distrust humans, where do you think they learned that behavior?

LEARNING THE MECHANICS

When you learn the mechanics of something, you have an easier time learning "the something." A good example would be when my husband David and I moved three hours away from snow skiing. We had both been ski instructors and decided to teach a class on cross country skiing at our local college.

Our "ski area" was a room with a wooden floor where we taught everyone to glide with wool socks. We used simulated video, humorous skits and fashion shows displaying proper clothing to wear once we made our first trip up to the mountain. For many of our students it was their first time on real snow. They were amazed how much easier it was to actually ski on their first lesson by learning the mechanics of skiing first. It was impressive. They learned to trust before they actually skied. It wasn't information overload. When they were on their skis for the first time they had a feel for what to expect.

In teaching 250 people this way for five years, we never had a serious injury and most of the people continued to ski afterward.

Learning to trust the mechanics of home cooking for your dog is similar. This book will not be telling you how much, how often or exactly what to feed **your** particular dog. I won't be giving you any recipes. Yogi will. He likes recipes. He's eaten many! That was a sign for me. I'd find paper bits in his poop the next day. He has a few good ones to share that are his favorites.

My suggestion would be to transfer Yogi's recipes to another piece of paper in your handwriting. Give the paper to your dog and see what he does with it. If he eats the paper, that's not a good sign. If he doesn't eat it, use it!

A lot of home cooking purists suggest no integration of commercial dog food and home cooking. It's that "all or nothing" attitude. If you're an experienced Dog Chef, go for it. My thinking is to be prepared for the big "if." I have experienced those power outages that lasted for days and spoiled meat. We've done cross country RV trips with our dogs to places like Wazoo City, Oklahoma, where a breakdown left us with very little choice of dog food.

This depends on you and your dog's lifestyle. If you seldom leave your home turf and just hang around your neighborhood, then free range, organic meat will do nicely. If you're retired or have plenty of free moments, food preparation time is not a problem. And if you have a cousin who lives near the Icelandic Sea, then have him ship you some cod liver oil, which is recommended in many home cooking books. The rest of us have to fit in what we can.

I chose the title of this book BECOMING THE CHEF YOUR DOG THINKS YOU ARE for a few reasons. First off, throughout the lifetime of your dog, his diet should be changing with his aging body. You will **always** be "becoming" a chef. If you are willing to learn, your dog will teach you.

Second, as a "chef," you can make the choice to home cook entirely, often, or just on weekends. You're not a short order cook. That can be dangerous for you and your dog. You're a serious chef, remember that. Learning to choose and handle meat for your dog is serious stuff.

Third, your dog thinks you're great no matter how often you cook for him. The more you do it the better the results. That will encourage you to continue the lifestyle.

Keep in mind the old adage, "It's not the destination, but the journey." This is another journey with our good pals that we will benefit from and remember for our lifetime. While we're "becoming" we're "being." That's what we are - human "beings." Most of us live our lives like human "doings" and our dog gets left out.

The final thought before we jump into the mechanics of home cooking is to remember one thing - your dog has a great stomach! We should all be envious of our dog's stomach. Listen to it, watch it (from the outside, of course) and see what comes out of it. That kind of observation will take you from amateur dog chef to Master Dog Chef in a short time.

We can learn from our feline friends to be patient and wait to see what happens when we give our dogs certain food. If the results are catastrophic, we probably won't want to repeat that again, or we may make it less concentrated, or mix or not mix it with something else.

Giving bones is a good example. They are not something we want to give our dog in large quantities until we know the results from a few trial runs.

Some dog stomach problems come from the dog eating soft, processed foods since he was a puppy. His stomach will take time to adjust and restore the proper bacteria he was given at birth. Slowly weaning your dog from his previous diet to a new one is the best approach.

Some people get very hung up with what their dog *should* eat versus what their dog *wants* to eat. If they read somewhere that turkey is good for dogs and they give it to their dog and the dog gives them a "no, thank you" look, my advice is to can it. Forget it. Take it off your list. Don't bother. I just gave you four ways to understand that your dog is **NOT** going to eat it! He's telling you that he doesn't like it - you're not hearing him.

What if I invite you over my house for a turkey dinner and I offer you white or dark meat and your preference is dark meat. I insist that white meat is better for you and I slam a piece of white meat on your plate and wait for you to eat it. You may eat it to be polite and gag afterwards or you may just refuse. Or you may even leave if I got too insistent. That's what your dog is doing. He may have taken a few bites because he trusts you and you've given him great things before, or he may just be polite.

Whatever the case, don't feed it to him anymore. It's that simple. Yogi loves turkey but he doesn't like turkey legs. Yogi never gets turkey legs. End of story.

Learning to make your life simpler and your dog healthier is the idea of this book. If you can't learn to let go of what the experts tell you and listen to what your dog is telling you, then continuing with this book will be a waste of your time.

Chapter Two will start with where I think many home cooking experiences go wrong. Not having a **butcher.** Here is a person who is more important than your vet when it comes to cooking for your dog. Your butcher will tell you more about meat then you ever wanted to know. A butcher is better than cod liver oil from the Icelandic Sea! He's in your neighborhood and he's a walking meat magnet!

Stop chasing your tail and find a butcher!

CHAPTER TWO

GETTING INTIMATE WITH A BUTCHER

When I was five years old I remember being horrified when I witnessed my grandmother plant a big kiss on the cheek of our local butcher. I accompanied her to the market. When we got to the meat counter, the big man with the funny hat and the blood-stained white apron came around the counter and hugged my grandmother while she proceeded to kiss him, from my point of view, longingly on the cheek.

My first thought was, "So long Grandpa." During those "intimate" moments with my grandmother and the butcher, I caught my first glimpse of "foreplay" for meat.

In front of my very eyes, I witnessed my grandmother transform from being the stern woman she was into a soft rose petal with minute drops of dew. Her dewy voice curled her words so delicately, I had to watch her lips to actually see if all of that conversation had originated from her.

The "foreplay" was short (butchers were busy guys in those days), not much more than a few minutes. The "climax" came when Grandma reached across the counter and took possession of a white paper-wrapped blob of meat.

In a few minutes we were headed for home, Grandma no longer soft and dewy. When my grandfather came home that evening I heard him ask my grandmother if she had seen the butcher that day. Bracing myself for the worse, I was surprised to hear her tell my grandfather the truth about their "intimacy".

"Yeah, I went there today. Got a half a pound extra meat and two bones for a kiss on his cheek." My grandmother blurted out.

"A half a pound extra? Are you sure all you did was kiss him on the cheek?"

I heard something hit the wall. I came around the corner to see my grandfather duck a flying apple.

"I'm just asking, 'cause Mrs. Modjewski says Ollie the butcher only gives extra when he gets extra."

Grandma took her hand and walloped my grandfather on the back of his bald head and walked out of the room. Grandpa saw me standing by the door, smiled and winked.

GETTING EXTRA...

My grandmother was not a "loose" woman but she knew the art of "getting extra". At subsequent visits with my grandmother, to see Ollie the butcher, I was no longer blinded by my fantasy of Grandma betraying Grandpa. I was being taught the art of "schmoozing".

It wasn't just with Ollie the butcher that Grandma schmoozed. She schmoozed all over town! At the bakery, she schmoozed differently then at the coal yard. I even caught her schmoozing with the rag man who came weekly through the alley way with his horse-drawn cart. She gave his horse Maple a carrot from her garden, he gave her a few cents extra for her papers.

At the bakery, pictures were looked at of the grandchildren, the new automobile or the latest wedding. At the coal yard the discussion went on about whose account had been closed because they died.

What I noticed was most of my grandparents' friends schmoozed on some level. The ones who did not, got what they paid for and that was all. The ones who schmoozed, got extra.

In today's world, schmoozing still goes on. We see more of it in familiar settings or small towns, but it is still a good way to enhance your daily commerce. People love to see a familiar face, someone they can relate to on some level.

MEETING YOUR BUTCHER

When clients consult with me about home cooking for their dog, our first lesson is to have them "meet their butcher." At first, most people are apprehensive about such a meeting and say they would rather not do it. I tell them that we are going to meet and talk with a butcher, not a priest. I also flatly refuse to go any further unless they do what I say and soon they relent.

Why is meeting your butcher so important? Because he is the one who can share many "secrets" with you. Just as my grandmother and Ollie the butcher used to do. After my grandmother's expected kiss,

Ollie took her aside and told her secrets about the best meat to purchase.

In my grandmother's day, meat contamination was a very big problem. Refrigeration was not what it is today so the preferable meat to purchase was from an animal that was recently slaughtered close by. Ollie knew those secrets plus other tidbits of information, like whose livestock was sick or how they were fed.

How important would those secrets be for us and our dogs today? Very important!

As far as we have advanced in the areas of refrigeration, transportation and cleaner and healthier sanitation standards, we still **need to know** the history behind the animal and its origins.

This does not mean that you need to have a lengthy discussion about the life of Beulah the cow and whether or not she was a vegan and practiced safe sex. The conversation can go as simply as, "This meat is fresh, free-ranged from Petaluma."

Or you may not even discuss the meats' origins but he might fill you in on a good deal he can get you on beef hearts.

You can be sure if there was ever a problem with meat, a local or national e-coli scare, or something that he thought you needed to watch out for, your pal, the butcher, would let you know.

A PICTURE IS WORTH A THOUSAND WORDS

I guarantee that you do not even have to kiss his or her cheek to get great service. A better way would be to bring a photo of your dog(s) with you to the store for the first time you meet your butcher. Tell him you are starting to home cook for your dog and you need his help to guide you through the initial "training" period of becoming the chef your dog thinks you are. Show him the picture of your dog and tell him that "Fredd" would be indebted to him for life.

Ask your butcher if he can bag up some loose meat ends or bones for you and "Fredd" (always use your dogs name frequently along with your name, that way your butcher will be able to make that association. Flash "Fredd's" photo whenever the opportunity arises).

Don't be concerned that your butcher might think you are nuts. I'm sure he will! He will tell the other butchers about you and you will more than likely make "story time" at his Thanksgiving Dinner. That is all part of schmoozing. You also will be sharing stories about "your butcher" and soon you will be sought out at parties from people who want to know how they too can get their "own butcher."

SIZING UP A BUTCHER

Ollie the butcher would probably not meet the standards of today's butcher, at least the ones **YOU** would be looking for. You want to know one who practices personal hygiene - in other words, they and where they work need to be **FRESH AND CLEAN!**

THE GOOD OLD DAYS OF BEING A BUTCHER

For forty-one years, Ernie Navone was a meat-magnet. At least that's the way most dogs looked at him. Fresh out of the Navy, Ernie asked himself, "What's next?" In lieu of continuing college, he got a job in his hometown stocking shelves at Keller's Market in the quiet town of St. Helena, CA. The year was 1949. Leo Keller, butcher man and owner of the market, knew a potential butcher when he saw one. Ernie had the right stuff. He was enthusiastic, willing to learn, and loved the customers. In fact, as Ernie puts it today, ten years after retirement, "That was the best part - the customers!"

Ernie loved to do anything for his customers. His criteria was, "If the customer was nice and not demanding, they could have anything in the world! If they wanted alligator meat, I'd find it for them. But, if they were pushy - forget it!" In fact, with his few "pushy" customers, Ernie told them he wouldn't be able to find the meat they were looking for, but that his competitor across the street, Elmer, would be able to help them. It wasn't long before Ernie found out that Elmer was doing the same thing! They were simply exchanging "pushy" customers!

In 1968, Ernie bought out the butcher shop of the market and called it Ernie's Meats. He was by then, the most popular man in town, the man to know!

Ernie sold a pet food that was made up of chicken backs, hearts and trimmings, ground up like hamburger. The townspeople came in weekly to buy up all he had for their pets.

"Our philosophy was simple, don't sell anything to anybody that you wouldn't eat yourself!" His pet food was included in that belief.

Ernie liked the idea of getting "intimate" with his customers. Building up a relationship with a customer was very rewarding. "I knew their kids, how many dogs or cats they had, I knew a lot about them. We were family."

Ernie says finding a good butcher should be simple. Use your eyes **and** your nose. The butcher himself should look clean. "That's the hardest part is staying and looking clean throughout the day. It's a dirty, bloody job but you want someone who is fastidious." Ernie goes on to say your nose should not be offended by the meat smell.

In Ernie's day as a butcher, the block where they cut the meat was scraped three to four times a day with a meat scraper and a final time at night when it was scrubbed down with bleach. They had an area to cut muscle meat and an area to cut chicken. That's required by law.

Asked how Ernie dealt with E-coli, his response was, "We never had any problem with it." The main reason was he got his meat from the local slaughter house only a few miles away. The slaughter house was owned by the Keller brothers, who also owned the store. The cattle were purchased live and brought to the Keller ranch where they were fed molasses, hay and oats for ten to thirty days before they were slaughtered.

Ernie proves that a relationship between you and your butcher is a necessary one when home cooking becomes a ritual. A butcher like Ernie will not only fulfill your dogs' greatest fantasies with food but he'll be nourishing **your** soul also.

"When I'd get a customer who was really in a hurry, I'd intentionally slow down. It was good for them." Ernie was good for a lot of us!

In Ernie's butcher days, cleanliness was as important as it is today. The difference is not so much in the butcher shop as it is in the transportation. Very few people live near a slaughter house. Most of us are happy about that. Because of our "not-in-my-backyard" attitude, we depend more on transporting meat from remote areas or clear across the country. Cows are now raised in massive herds where the butcher himself never sees the cow or even the carcass any longer.

Besides the mishandling of raw food in our own home, transporting meat, from the slaughter house to the butcher shop, is where our bacteria problems like e-coli begin. This is where your relationship with a butcher has the most advantages, even in a large chain store meat market.

If you're under forty years old, you have probably never seen a single butcher shop that was not housed within a large chain store. Today, our choices are limited to a small neighborhood store with a tiny meat market or a large chain store with a huge meat market. Or, you may be lucky to live in an area where you have a large natural food chain store like Whole Foods or Wild Oats, selling free range and organic meats in their meat market. Also, farmers' markets are now allowing organic meats to be sold at their weekly venue.

If you have some land of your own, raising your own chickens, sheep, cows or pigs might be something that appeals to the back-to-the-land crowd. Of course, raising them is one thing, slaughtering them is another!

SCHMOOZING WITH A SUPERMARKET BUTCHER

Getting a butcher's attention in a supermarket or making him come out from behind the glass room adjacent to the rows of cut meat takes an advanced course in schmoozing. Many of us are familiar with "the bell." It protrudes over the row of meat with a small sign saying "Ring For Assistance." When you ring "the bell" a butcher comes out to help you.

When I have interviewed clients about home cooking for their dogs, most of them have expressed a hesitancy toward ringing "the bell." It is rather disconcerting. You stand in the aisle talking to the butcher while he's usually holding the door partially open - a subtle hint to you that he is very busy so you better get on with it. If you're lucky, you might be able to accost one stacking meat in the counters.

I tell my clients to do several things. Ring "the bell." When a butcher comes out, step several feet away from the door. Make them come to you. If they still act like they are too busy to talk with you, take a hint from Ernie's story and "talk slower." If you slow down, they will have to slow down.

If they absolutely will not schmooze with you, then be polite and say, "Is there someone else in your glass room that is not so busy?"

Don't burn your bridges and blow up at them. They've seen it a million times.

It's best to be the exception. I've had encounters with chain store butchers who were not receptive the first time, but upon seeing me on the next trip, they've gone out of their way to greet me and help me out. Their conscience got the best of them because I schmoozed and they didn't.

In interviewing many butchers, rudeness and arrogance are their daily fare. If you restrain yourself from such behavior, they will not forget you.

Even though talking with customers and helping the customer is a butcher's job, it does not mean that they will do it willingly. I can't blame them sometimes.

Whether you're shopping at a small neighborhood butcher shop or a large chain store meat market, learning how to schmooze is right up there with what meat to buy for your dog.

THERE'S A SCHMOOZER BORN EVERY MINUTE

Every minute of every day, a schmoozer is born in this world. Really. I can't recall where I got that statistic but trust me, it's true. A schmoozer walks differently. Not graceful, but smooth and with a gait, like - well like your dog!

Our dogs are wonderful schmoozers. Think about it, you do things for them just because they give you their paw or just because they come when you ask. Don't tell me you don't have any role-model schmoozers, you live with one!

Spend some time studying your dog and his daily schmoozing, then go out and practice the same thing on your butcher. Treating someone like your dog treats you is prime meat! It's the best!

WHAT MAKES A GOOD SCHMOOZER?

Think about the people you know in your life who always seem to get something extra. The people who get a pair of free concert tickets to a sold-out concert or a free load of chicken manure delivered right to their home. How did they do that? They asked for it - **in a nice way.**

Sometimes we know schmoozers who are turn offs to us. We know the type that is always trying to get something for nothing. I'm not talking about those people. I'm talking about the schmoozer who practices the behavior closest to your dog's. We never feel like we've been schmoozed by our dog because he does it so subtly, so nicely. He gives us something in return.

In exchange for schmoozing us, our dog gives us kind eyes, a wet kiss, or slobber, in Yogi's case. They perform for us or make us laugh. A beginning schmoozer needs only to watch the master, his dog, for schmoozing hints.

When you schmooze with your butcher, he will schmooze back. Butchers know this stuff. They recognize schmoozing because they've been trained to spot it. If you happen to find a butcher who appears to be schmooze-illiterate, find another. If he doesn't know it by now, I guarantee he never will.

APPROPRIATE SCHMOOZING

It may take you and your new butcher a while to become familiar with each other's schmooze techniques. This is your "courting period." I call that **PRE-IN- SYNC-SCHMOOZING.**

You and your butcher will court for a bit before any serious schmoozing can occur. That's only natural. He's going to be paying attention to whether you're just a one-time schmooze or whether you are a regular schmooze. You're going to be deciding if he's on the same schmooze level as you.

Schmoozing has changed over the years since my grandmother used her schmoozing skills. The obvious change has come with what can be misinterpreted as "sexual harassment," whether it's with males or females. Very few people today can plant a kiss on a butcher's cheek as my grandmother did with Ollie, the butcher, and consider that schmoozing. More than likely, it will appear as something else.

Today, appropriate schmoozing is common courtesy with a dash of spice.

Talking about the weather is a good place to start, but move from there right away. That's schmoozing 101. Step into the intermediate course after two visits.

Carrying your dog's picture may seem silly but your new-found butcher friend will remember you on sight. It also sends a subtle message to him that you have an agenda. That's understood with advanced schmoozers and is not insulting.

I have a client who felt silly carrying his dog's photo with him each time he went to the meat market. He went to Kinko's and had the dog's photo copied onto a large button which he proudly wears when he shops. Now everyone in the store knows him and his dog. He has left the store with extra dog bones, dog dishes, collars and dog treats, saved for him by the store's personnel. When the store clears out products to bring others in, they think of Jake and his dog "Marvin." Jake usually ends up taking most of what extras he gets to the local animal shelter. Here's a guy who learned well from his dog Marvin in the art of schmoozing.

DRAWING THE SCHMOOZING LINE

When you subtly let your butcher know that you are schmoozing with him because of your dog, then the intent becomes clear to him and yourself. The line is now drawn. Let the schmoozing begin. As long as the intent remains obvious, the interpretation of your schmoozing will never get confused.

Ask your butcher about meat, he'll love it. You are genuinely interested in his business. He gets to blow his horn about his meat knowledge and you get to learn about the meat and gain from his knowledge. If you genuinely show interest, he will genuinely want to share the best he has to offer to you that day.

Butchers have better meat for their better customers and lesser meat for the others. That's human nature. Consider your business or your job. Maybe you have an opportunity to do the same thing. You take care of your better clients and give less to the ones who are rude or are just there.

My favorite four words are: **CAN YOU HELP ME?"** I have never met anyone who could resist that question. Even in foreign countries and even saying it in English, no one has yet to turn me down. There must be something to the pleading look that comes with it that translates into a magnetic and genuine appeal for help.

When we ask that question, we are entrusting our vulnerability to the other person. It's the same appeal that our dog does to us when he's sitting in the kitchen "asking"us for food, or a treat or a walk. You can't turn him down, even if you're busy.

Asking that of your butcher before he says, "Can I help you?"gives you the upper hand in the vulnerable end of things. It makes him perk up and invites him to genuinely get involved, no matter how busy he is.

Here's an example:

You walk into the butcher shop and he's busy cutting and wrapping meat. He recognizes that you are standing at the counter. He makes the first exchange.

"Can I help you?"

You say, "Yes, I'm looking for what's on special today."

He points to a tray of meat and returns to cutting his meat. He glances back to see if you have made up your mind. You say, "I'd like a pound of your special please."

He wraps the meat and thanks you and you leave.

The way our dogs would suggest you do it is when the butcher first recognizes you at the counter, you smile and ask, "Can you help me?"

"Sure, how can I help you?" You'll notice he's fully engaged in the conversation and forgets about the meat he was cutting.

"My dog, Yogi, has a big appetite. Tell me about your specials today, what do you think would be best for my buddy?" You've said a lot in those two sentences.

You've told him that you're shopping mainly for your dog. You're interested in his specials, but need his help to figure out what would be best for your good "buddy." You've made him "responsible" for taking good care of your best friend. If you had your dog's picture or had a photo button of your dog like Jake, that would reinforce the "responsibility."

The conversation can go into how often he has specials, what day of the week is the best to stop by and get bones, or any number of questions that pertain to meat for your dog.

If fish is something you feed occasionally, you can ask when he is expecting a fresh shipment and what days are best to buy fish. (Usually toward the end of the week, never buy fish on Mondays! Most people and restaurants buy fish for the weekend, for get togethers or holidays. Most of the time, those events don't take place on the first or middle part of the week. The exception would be along the coastal areas where fish is brought in fresh and in large quantities. You can get great deals at that time, and it will be highly advertised or a sign put up in the window of the store or meat market.)

Before you leave, drop a hint that you will be coming back again in a few days. Do that for several visits until he recognizes you and your needs. Your butcher sees a lot of customers and they all become a blur, except for you. He won't forget your trust, your genuine interest in his job, his responsibility to your best friend, or your photo button of your dog. Tell him how much your dog loved the last meal and that you told him you were leaving him at home (or in the car) to go see the "nice butcher man." Now he's "the nice butcher man." He will have to live up to that title.

One of the most important parts of schmoozing is this: keep your conversation light, quick, and about your dog and the butcher. This is not a place for you to complain, air out your differences in politics or religion or to talk about yourself. In exchange for your schmoozing and receiving something extra you have not said a word about yourself. You are giving your butcher the opportunity to shine, and you have **nourished** his soul and yours at the same time.

THE SUPER-DUPER MARKET AND YOUR DOG

Do you think schmoozing will end with the change from big supermarkets to super-duper markets? In one way, Yogi and I think so. It has changed since my grandmother and I stepped foot into Ollie's butcher shop.

After talking with several large chain supermarkets, the future of shopping as we know it will disappear. Some of the charm of shopping we haven't seen in awhile will return. A few of the larger chain stores are listening to their customers, modernizing their stores, and improving the technology at the same time they are recreating a butcher shop of old.

There will be more "ready-prepared" meals, not frozen, but packaged fresh and dated, to take home, heat and eat. Your dog's food will be purchased that way also.

There's talk of child care facilities in grocery stores to encourage the harried mother to do all her shopping in one place. Will there be doggy care facilities too, so the harried dog owner doesn't have to worry about his dog in a hot car? Or maybe there will be pet markets, that just sell freshly packaged pet food specifically for your dog to fit his size, his age, his health?

We will always have to schmooze, in some way or another. It is part of our make up, especially if we live with dogs. They are the master schmoozers. We will demand more from the places where we will be buying our food, and we will be attracted to those places that remind us of what nourishes us. As Dog Chefs, we'll sniff it out.

CHAPTER THREE

Saving Face and Telling Your Dog the Truth About Commercial Dog Food

This is going to be hard. Harder then cleaning out your dog's ears. Probably harder then squeezing his anal sacs. If you are going to go through with your apprenticeship of being your dog's chef, you can't skip this chapter. It's inevitable. You **will** have to face him and see the hurt in his eyes. You **will** have to tell him where his "food" came from and what it's made of, but hey - he loves you! Forgiveness is a dog's middle name. Besides, he knew it all along, he was waiting for you to catch on.

My dog, Tonto, told me that the reason that dogs bury their bones is because they know bones are real food. When dogs are not getting **real food** they can dig up a bone to nourish themselves. You might want to check your back yard and see if your dog has buried a lot of bones. If he has, you'll **need** to have that inevitable talk with him right away. This chapter will give you some ideas about how to talk with your dog and let him know that **real food** will be making its way into his bowl from now on.

WHERE DOES DOG FOOD COME FROM?

Picture the perfect farm with free range cows and horses, lambs, and little squealing piggies, foraging among lush acres of grass. Near the perfect farmhouse are chickens roosting here and there, cackling away in the mid-day sun. A wonderful wave of smells come out of the farmhouse kitchen. The farmer's wife puts two luscious homemade apple pies on the window ledge as she heads out to the barnyard to feed her chickens freshly ground corn, apple cores, and peelings.

Now, picture your average bag or can of dog food. Does it say anywhere on the label: free range, freshly slaughtered cows, (horses!), lambs, squealing piggies, and well fed chickens? Or freshly ground corn, oats, bulgur, rice, etc.?

If you're still buying regular commercial dog food from big chain stores or even mom and pop stores, or if you're buying some of the more expensive *designer* dog food, and the majority or the first ten ingredients are not from the picture of your perfect farm, you've got a lot of explaining to do to your dog.

He's going to want to know what a poultry by-product meal is? Or he might ask about meat and bone meal and animal by-product meal. Do you have some pictures of these things to show your dog what they look like? How about corn gluten meal? Ground grain sorghum?

Do **you** really know what a sorghum is? Can you identify a sorghum field if you passed it, and point it out to your dog? You'd better be prepared to answer some difficult questions.

The majority of commercial dog food is comprised of processed foods, synthetic vitamins and minerals, and chemical preservatives that most of us would have a difficult time picking out in a line-up, even if our life depended on it!

Dogs all over the country are asking, "What is this stuff? And where does it come from?"

It's a long way from your picture of the perfect farm. At one time, most of it was food in some pathetic state or another. How many eons ago was it processed before it made its way to your dog's dish?

THE HISTORY OF COMMERCIAL DOG FOOD - (KINDA)

Commercial dog food has a very short history in the lives of humans on this planet. In the time line of evolution, commercial dog food as we know it today, has only been with us for a split second. Or, as your dog would say, "a burp or a fart" in the space of evolution.

Depending whose recall you are dealing with, commercial dog food has been around for forty to sixty years. Within that short period of time, we humans have let ourselves become convinced we are totally incapable of creating meals for our dogs, despite feeding ourselves and perhaps our family, on a daily basis.

Somehow, before the advent of commercial dog food, people managed to adequately feed their pets and themselves. It is reasonable to suggest that many people do not feed themselves and their families very well. Their diets leave a lot to be desired. That hasn't changed in the history of man. (In caveman days, fast food and bad diets were prevalent. It wasn't unusual to see cavemen standing in line for brontosaurus burgers. The accuracy of that information can be challenged since I got it from watching the Flintstones.)

Truly, not every caveman was capable of killing a mastodon. Life as a human is just that way. So what else is new?

That's what our dogs would like to know? **What else is new?** Humans have not gotten dumber in the last 40 years, just lazier and/or busier. Feeding your dog home prepared meals is easier than feeding yourself, or feeding kids or elderly people. The health requirements for you, your kids and your elderly parents are more complicated then your dog's.

If you have taken the time to read this book, you have already made your dog a member of your family and not just another pet. You don't tell a member of your family that eating the same thing everyday out of a can or a bag is good for them and will keep them **vitally** healthy. If you do, shame on you. I suspect you don't and from now on you won't "tell" your dog that either.

No one knows for sure, but Americans spend somewhere around $11 billion per year on commercial pet food. That's a profitable gravy train!

In the last 10 years or so, the pet food industry has stepped up to another level of dog food and increased their profits along the way. Like designer jeans, **designer** dog food has appealed to the person who figures you get what you pay for. With designer jeans you have someone's name embroidered on your butt. With designer dog food, you got a better quality of food **condemned** for human consumption.

If you are feeding your dog designer dog food, don't feel bad. Each one of us Master Dog Chefs did that at some point in our evolution.

Although it took many years to focus the spotlight, once the hoopla settled down about how great designer dog food was, the scrutiny began. What many dog-lovers found out was for the fistful of dollars they were paying, they were still getting highly processed, chemically preserved pet food, most of which was still coming from a **rendering** plant and not fit for human consumption. Such scrutiny is changing the industry, which is a good thing for our dogs.

In the last ten years, dog-lovers have sniffed out many inappropriate ingredients in dog food. My favorite, which is still in several inexpensive and a few expensive pet foods, is ethoxyquin. Ethoxyquin is used to extend the shelf life in pet foods **and** some human foods. I recently saw it on the label of an inferior brand of cayenne pepper. The ingredient list read: cayenne pepper, ethoxyquin.

I suppose Monsanto, the company that created ethoxyquin, must have thought they hit a vein of gold when they came up with the idea of promoting ethoxyquin to the pet food industry to extend the shelf life of dog food. After all, it worked on tires! Yes, tires. Ethoxyquin did such a great job of keeping tires from drying out from sunlight and the elements that it was only natural it would be put in your dog's food. Why didn't I think of that?

I didn't think of that because it would be the last thing I would consider as real food. Over ten years ago, ethoxyquin was on the FDA's ten worst list for carcinogens. All of a sudden, it's status changed and it made its way into pet and human food. Who'd a thunk it?

I caution you, many people, including some veterinarians, defend the use of ethoxyquin and other chemical preservatives. If you don't want chemicals in your dog's food, then decide to ignore their defense of them. It's like going to a hairdresser who wears a beehive hairdo. If you're not into beehive hairdos, you may choose another hairdresser. Choose another vet.

TAILS FROM A RENDERING PLANT

Your dog's not going to like this. A discussion about **rendering** plants always raises hackles, even in humans.

I have never been to a rendering plant and do not personally know anyone who has. The stories abound of them on the Internet, in books, among veterinarians, dog food competitors, and pet lovers. Butchers have very graphic stories to tell of them. As a Dog Chef, you **must** know about rendering plants in order to make wise decisions about your dog's food. The following is the "cleanest" version I can give you. I won't belabor the subject, in hopes that you will continue to research rendering plants and how they can affect yours and your families lives, for better or for worse.

Rendering is the process of cooking "raw" (dead) animal material, to remove the moisture and fat. The rendering plant works like a giant kitchen. The cooker, blends the raw (dead) product in order to maintain a certain ratio between the carcasses of pets, livestock, poultry waste and supermarket rejects.

This mass is then cut into small pieces and transported to another auger for fine shredding. Non-stop, twenty-four hours a day, seven days a week, a continuous batch is cooked at 280 degrees for an hour. Meat melts away from bones in the hot "soup," producing a fat of yellow grease or tallow that rises to the top and is skimmed off. A hammer mill press, squeezes out the remaining moisture and pulverizes the cooked meat and bones into a gritty powder. Once each batch is finished, yellow grease, meat and bone meal is what's left.

This recycled source of protein then goes into the diets of poultry and swine and in to pet foods. Lesser amounts are used in the food of cattle and sheep, where it is mixed with other ingredients to feed billions of animals that meat-eating humans, in turn, will eat.

Rendering plants recycle dead animals. That's a very valuable function for our planet. Think about it. Without rendering plants, cities would be filled with diseased and rotting animal carcasses. Fatal viruses and bacteria would spread uncontrolled through the population. Rendering plants must be horrible, but without them our planet would be in a serious state of decay.

ONLY MAD DOGS ...

The phrase, "Only mad dogs and Englishmen go out in the noonday sun," was used to describe foolhardy behavior. Recycling dead animal carcasses for food has been an ongoing practice for many years. The foolhardy behavior that concerns me is all that goes into "the pit" where the dead animals are shoved; flea collars still attached to the pet that wore it, cattle arrive with insecticide patches of Dursban, antibiotics in livestock, euthanasia drugs given to pets, and a variety of heavy metal sources, such as pet ID tags, surgical pins and needles. Even plastic winds up going into the pit. Unsold and rotten supermarket meats, chicken, and fish arrive in Styrofoam trays, and shrink wrap and plastic bags containing dead pets from veterinarians - all are tossed into the pit.

Skyrocketing labor makes it too costly for plant personnel to cut off flea collars or unwrap millions of weekly packages of plastic-wrapped meat. Rendering plants have reached the horrors of a Stephen King novel.

Most pet food companies deny that they buy rendered products as an additive or as the main ingredient for their food. Then where do they get their chicken (poultry) by-product or bone meal or animal by-product meal? The amount of pet food sold in this country and the listing of these ingredients on their packaging can only lead to a small amount of sources. As a Dog Chef, not a short order cook, most of us would rather not **trust** the large pet food companies. Their food production is not designed with your dog's **vibrant** health and **nourishment** in mind.

The other end of this Stephen King novel on rendering plants is the labeling of a particular "run" of product defined by the predominance of a specific animal(s). "Animal by-products"is made from any rendered animal tissue, that includes road kill, dogs, cats, cattle, sheep, etc., anything animal. If you serve your dog a food made with this product listed on the label, this is what they are getting. You can find this on the labels of many of the inferior dog foods, but it has shown up on labels of occasional designer dog foods, spotted by ever-watching dog lovers.

In Britain, in 1985, more than 160,000 cases of "mad cow disease" were confirmed. This degenerative neural disease came from the practice of supplementing cows' food with the ground-up nervous tissue and offal of sheep and other cattle.

Cows stricken with the disease exhibit behavioral problems, and over time their brains degenerate. In 1989, British authorities banned the practice of feeding rendered animal parts, which resulted in a decreased incidence of mad cow disease from 36,000 cases in 1992 to 14,000 in 1995. But, the nightmare returned a few years later when the British government announced the findings of a new strain of Creutzfeld-Jakob Disease (CJD) in humans, and suggested mad cow disease as a possible cause. Scientists know little about CJD, which causes symptoms similar to Alzheimer's disease.

The CJD had generally been restricted to an average age of sixty-three, but scientists were shocked to find more recent cases averaging twenty-nine years of age. Analyses are complicated because CJD appears to have a fifteen year incubation period.

In the United States, farmers are allowed to feed rendered cow and other animal parts to cows. About 14 percent of cow carcasses are used as dietary supplements for cattle.

Is this prudent husbandry or do only mad dogs and Englishmen go out in the noon day sun?

WHAT IS REAL FOOD?

If you're looking for your dog, he's probably raiding the refrigerator right now. After hearing the truth about his food, he's willing to eat just about anything that doesn't come in a bag or a can.

Master Dog Chefs follow the laws of Nature, which are not subject to opinion or variance. They let **truth** be their authority and not authority be their truth. A healthy, vibrant dog is disease free. Disease is the effort of the body to keep the body alive. That's where **real food** comes in. Real food is compatible with the body and lends itself to the building up of health and maintaining life. It contains nothing that is harmful, toxic or non usable by the body.

I define **real food** as that which is provided by Nature in the form of fruits, vegetables and animals which have not been processed or altered in any way. Cooking alters food, and that will be discussed further in the next chapter. Have you ever caught a glimpse of a coyote in the wild cooking his food over a camp fire? Or a fox or any carnivore? The closest we've come is with a raccoon who spends time washing his food.

Cooking changes the molecular structure of food. It binds food molecules tighter together, making them more difficult to digest and making the food unfamiliar to the dog's body.

Every Dog Chef I have interviewed has a reason or a belief for their home prepared meals. Many **cook** their dog's food, many do not. I find many Dog Chefs rely on the "breed specific" plan. Where did the original dog's breed come from? What country? What food were they fed there? What was the purpose of their existence, what was their job? Even if your dog is a mutt, he resembles some breed.

Real food can mean different things to different dogs or "one dog's meat is another's poison."

The main idea is to get you away from **entirely** feeding commercial dog food to your dog. To supplement his diet with **real food** is certainly better than nothing.

THINK PREY

If your dog was living in the wild, (pre-domestication) he would be spending his day like his ancestor the wolf - having a purpose. Instead of licking his butt or biting at flies, his down time would be spent resting up for the hunt, the hunt for prey to be exact. If prey was scarce that day, then he would forage on insects, eggs, and plants.

Let's say today is your "wild" dog's lucky day. He's sitting in a field daydreaming, when a large jackrabbit just about stumbles over his tail. For an instant "Jeffro" can't believe his eyes but his stomach is already sending him the cue to step on the gas and bring home the bacon! Go, Jeffro, go! At this moment, Jeffro is "thinking prey." He is zeroed in on the rabbit, bobbing and weaving with his new-found energy. Meanwhile, his stomach juices are preparing for the expected meal. Jeffro, still running, is salivating.

This time Jeffro wins. He takes the rabbit down. After catching his breath and sniffing the prey, he bites into the stomach. He may eat the stomach contents, depending on preference, hydrating himself with the liquid. He may eat the organs, also depending on his like or dislike or how much he may have had in previous catches. He certainly will eat the muscle meat and dine on the bones and flesh, also consuming the fat.

When you're thinking real food for your dog, **think prey**. If your dog was living in the wild, prey to him would be birds, rabbits, mice, rats, and fish, along with insects, eggs, plants, and nuts.

Living in your home, prey for your dog would be meat and fish, along with eggs, grains, vegetables and even some nuts. And for many dogs - bones.

Thinking prey will lead you to thinking **fresh, live foods.** These foods are essential to the health of your dog (and yourself), because they are **enzyme-active** and have not had their nutritional substances

destroyed or altered by heat or processing. Your dog's body can **utilize** these foods.

With processed dog food, his body has to figure out what to do with these chemically-altered foods, making his digestion work harder to find places in the body to store the excess. A typical SADD (Standard American Dog Diet) is usually processed for long-term storage requirements. Live **enzymes** are totally lost, reducing assimilation of nutrients. Also, many of the vitamins and minerals have been destroyed or altered.

Your dog's body can be maintained from his SAD diet, but his nutrient needs for peak health are not met. He will age prematurely.

We, Master Dog Chefs, can't stomach that!

"QUESTIONITIS"

Questionitis is a treatable "disease" that many beginner Dog Chefs contract. The "symptoms" are varied, but the questions are the same. "Exactly how much? How often? When should I do that? Who can I ask?" The incessant need to know, the need for constant reassurance, the need to ask someone of authority are the other symptoms.

There is only one cure for **questionitis.** Take action, do it, drop it like a hot potato! Learn to be "becoming," not to "be." None of us are "being" Dog Chefs, we all <u>are,</u> and forever will be "becoming" Dog Chefs. When your present dog dies, you will start all over again with your next dog, always "becoming."

You will reach Master Dog Chef status, but that will only be in the areas of schmoozing and the mechanical end of preparing home meals for your pet. Your previous dog might have been a St. Bernard, now you have a Chihuahua. Big difference, little dog.

The need for an authority figure to sanction your every move is disappointing for your dog. **HE** is the **ONLY** authority figure worth his weight, give the rest the raspberry! Every dog is individual. To take someone's idea of the best diet for your dog is silly. You live with him, you smell his farts, you hear him burp, you watch him poop. You even step in his poop and know how much he poops and when. You know if he eats poop! You know this stuff, you don't have to ask anyone, you know it by heart.

That is **how** your dog is **telling** you about himself. He lets you watch him poop, or step in it, or he unashamably farts in your face. Or he runs out and hurriedly eats grass or wood or plain old dirt. He's telling you everything you need to know about him every day. That's plain old **dog talk.**

I've always been amused when talking with clients who have consulted with me about their dog's diet. They come down with an early case of "questionitis" and I suggest to them that they need to listen to what their dog is telling them. A week later, the questionitis has gotten worse, and I ask them if they have been "listening" to their dog?

They reply in a way that sounds like they actually expect their dog will literally speak to them! When we go over what they can expect to **hear** from their dog, they are surprised and say, "Oh, I know that, he's done this and this since he was a puppy!" Another disease is cured!

When you decide for yourself what sort of meal you are going to have for dinner (barring any strange diets you might be on), do you measure your proportions and figure the percentages of nutrients before you eat your food? Basically, you take the whole day in perspective. Where are you when sitting down for dinner? Are you in a hurry? Relaxed? How hungry are you? What did you do all day? Lay around? Run around? Dig up your yard? What did you eat earlier? Meat? Fruit? Veggies? Did you make homemade bread and eat 5 slices? What's missing in your food plan for that day?

Now, forget about yourself and put your dog in the picture. Ask the same questions. It may appear that you're having a reoccurrence of questionitis again, but you're not. The questions you're asking are to yourself about your dog. You answer them from what he **told** you that day, or the day before.

If he was "talking" like my dog Tonto, then you would understand that bones are his main staple. Watching when he's not eating bones tells you that he needs other food for that day.

Yogi tells me he needs more nourishment when he's chasing cats that day or chasing himself. That's Yogi's way of talking. Your dog may chase cats because he likes to chase cats. Put two and two together. Try to figure out a pattern, if you don't see one, then it's not there!

Questionitis can reoccur often, especially the first year that it is contracted. You will have to learn how to identify the symptoms.

Becoming a Master Dog Chef requires that you "become" a **dog food detective.** You know you have become a dog food detective and not come down with another case of questionitis when you focus on what your dog has told you that day, as opposed to what you think your dog needs. Or what you read, or what someone with three Dobermans told you.

I have a simple solution for you. Go to a nature store or catalog and buy a small magnifying glass. Tie it around your neck and when you feel the symptoms of questionitis start to surface, walk around the yard following your dog, looking through the magnifying glass.

It will all come very clear to you, I guarantee it!

TABLE SCRAP VS TABLE CRAP

Here's food for thought. To find out what food might be good for your dog to eat that comes directly off your table, drop the "s" in the word "table scrap." That makes the word "table crap."

Table scraps are not all bad. It depends on what **your** diet is like.

If you eat healthy, fresh, live foods, feeding your dog from the table can be part of his chuck wagon. If your idea of nouvelle cuisine is hamburgers and french fries, that's table crap for your dog. Don't bother. Unfortunately, many people define table scraps as "home prepared" meals for their dog. Table scraps can be supplements for your dog's home prepared meal or they can add life to a SAD diet.

Table scraps should not be your dog's entire enchilada when it comes to his daily diet. If you are supplementing his commercial dog food, then table scraps could be 25 to 50% of his daily intake. Obviously, when supplementing your dog's food with **healthy** scraps from your table, you will be cutting down on the portions of commercial dog food. Right? That's a **common sense test!**

Food from our table can be another way of nourishing our dog **and** our soul. Dining with our dogs is a healthy experience, as long as the food lives up to the experience. Left over veggies, rice, boiled potatoes, rare meat or chicken without the grease - these are all healthy table scraps.

Remember to **think prey.** That chicken fried steak swimming in grease is nowhere close to its original state. It no longer contains the enzymes or nutrients it had before it went into the frying pan. You will do more harm than good feeding your dog such table crap.

SHOULD YOUR DOG GO VEGGIE?

Yogi and I are often asked if a dog can live as a vegetarian? We look at each other and both of us have the same thought. **Have you asked your dog?** When you give him meat, does he turn away and cringe? Does he vomit after eating meat, raw or otherwise? What kind of dog is he? Is he a German Shepherd or a wolf hybrid? Do you know where he was born or his previous eating habits?

Yogi says he can not live **well** as a vegetarian, but some dogs can and do. Dogs have human-like metabolisms and do not necessarily require animal products in their **daily** meals.

Yogi's best friend is one of my six cats named Bungi. Cats are **obligate** carnivores. They literally are obligated to eat meat. Their bodies are unable to produce certain nutrients found only in animal products. Bungi has a slogan that fits his life, "a mouse a day keeps the vet away." Bungi is seven years old and has never returned to the vet since

his initial visit and shots.

Though dogs are omnivores and can **exist** without daily portions of meat, there are many types of dogs that need meat daily, such as German Shepherds or wolf hybrids.

Here's where **common sense** and **nourishment** play a big role in your becoming the chef your dog thinks you are. Let's pretend you are a "real" chef for humans. You have your own restaurant and a call comes in for you to have a special dinner for twenty people of the Orthodox Jewish faith. Common sense tells you that this will not be an ordinary dinner. If you are not familiar with appropriate foods for people of the Jewish faith you will investigate and research further. At the same time you are concerned about nourishing these people to the extent that they will feel satisfied and return to your restaurant again.

Common sense tells us that if we want our dogs to be vegetarians then we must research and investigate his background further. We also must ask ourselves why we want our dogs to be vegetarians? Is it for us, because we are vegetarians? Does the thought of handling meat make you want to up chuck your bean sprouts?

Several years ago, I would have felt your pain - or nausea. No longer. Yogi eats raw meat and will for the rest of his life. We skip a meal once a week for fasting.

I am no longer a strict vegetarian, but I do recall the "meat handling" dilemma. The thought of handling meat if you don't eat it yourself, or the killing of animals as food are two ethical problems of vegetarians. I can tell you how I dealt with it and you will have to make that decision on your own.

IT'S TOUGH TO BE A VEGETARIAN

If you have investigated ingredients as much as I have and researched their origins you would be shocked to find out where they came from and what they **really** are. During the Industrial Age of our society, we have become efficient at making use (good or bad) of animal wastes. These wastes show up in a variety of products and are made from beef products, such as: biscuit and bread, desserts, potato chips and other snack foods, lipstick and gelatin-based nutritional products. I recently found a sunscreen that had an ingredient that is traced back to a beef origin.

Unless you buy everything from a total vegetarian environment, you will not be living total vegetarianism. Some vegetarians tell me they buy most of their products from a health food store. Give me less then a one minute stroll down their aisles and I'll show you products galore that have beef origins. It's tough being a vegetarian, consequentially most vegetarians really are not.

It's also tough living in a world where most everything, except wood, plastic, metal and stone, are made from animal hides and carcasses. We can reject the killing of animals for food, but have a very difficult time not wearing clothes, driving in our cars and using products that are created, in some way, from animal products.

There are also the issues of taking pharmaceuticals or using health products that are tested on animals. The parade is endless, but not hopeless.

It's tough being a human vegetarian but more so if you're a dog.

What if you have strong vegetarian beliefs and you live with a German Sheppard? Yogi and I would suggest to you that there are human vegetarian chefs who prepare meat meals. Handling meat for your dog will not make you a hypocrite. It may make you nauseous, and if it does then you have three choices. You can:

1.) make good use of your imagination while you are handling meat and think about something else, which is what I do. 2.) You can hire someone to cut meat for you where all you have to do is put it in your friend's bowl. You can also have frozen dog food meat shipped to your house on a weekly basis (See Resource Guide). Or 3.) you can make your dog a vegetarian.

Number three is harder but not impossible, and there are a few good commercial dog food products made for vegetarian dogs and their people and more coming on the horizon.

Feeding your dogs home prepared vegetarian meals requires more thinking on your part. One of the problems that can surface is the overuse of grains. There is so much talk about dogs and their overeating of grains that it leaves most of us in a pickle. Allergy-sensitive dogs will communicate their dislike of grains by itching and scratching to excess. Hot spots and excessive chewing on paws or legs are also ways to decipher their language. And obesity.

We have become so indoctrinated with the use of grains as humans that we have transferred our belief to our best friends. The controversy about grains for humans and dogs is explosive. With dogs, we have become so "ingrained" with the idea of using them as a staple that even hard core home cooking pros have a difficult time leaving grains back in the field.

I have wrestled with the grain issue for years. I have come to terms with it as a human by eating fewer grains. Talk about hard going at first. Now, two years later, I feel healthier and have created a world where I eat them only on occasion at someone elses house or in a restaurant.

It's taken me longer to part company from grains as far as my pets are concerned. I've had to take it step by step and logically look at where my discomfort of this "comfort" food comes from. All fingers point to commercial pet food companies. (They make such great scapegoats!)

When you read the ingredients on a bag of dog food, what is the bulk of the contents? Grains. What is the most inexpensive ingredient in the bag? Grains. What is the hardest ingredient in the bag for your dog to digest? Grains.

Most **people** have been raised on opening a bag of dog food and pouring out golden nuggets of a grain mixture and not seeing chickens, turkeys and cows in the flesh. Grains are comfort food to us. When we are depressed we binge on potato chips and snack foods and pasta, not steak and eggs.

Because we love our dogs, we want them to "feel" as comforted as we do when eating grains. So grains have become, in our minds, the symbol of good nutrition.

Maybe, maybe not. The lines are being drawn, the battle (that is already being fought behind the scenes) will soon begin on home soil.

The biggest toll will be on the businesses that have been creating products exclusively with grains. With the changes in this new century, no one will be left untouched. Each and every one of our lives and those of our pets, will have to go through some sort of "recurrent training," a dramatic change in the way we have been doing everything.

For the most of us, feeding our dogs the way we have in the last forty - fifty years **will** change, in some way. Food will become more customized, more individualized. So there is hope for the vegetarian and the vegetarian dog. Your life will be getting easier.

This is where I would choose to part company. I chose to be Yogi's chef. His metabolism does best on meat, I handle his meat. In the end, as a vegetarian, this is your choice and the fact that you have **chosen** to read this book makes me confident that you will be becoming the best chef for your dog that you can be, with or without meat.

CHEW ON THIS

As a Dog Chef, I would prefer to buy my dog's food locally. If that's not always possible and I'm buying some form of commercial dog food, my second choice would be to have the food delivered to my house as fresh as it can be without sitting on a shelf for who knows how long. Third, I would go to a local feed store or pet specialty store and with my chef magnifying glass, look for the manufacturing date on the bag or can. If you can't find or interpret the date, ask. Be snoopy.

Snoopy was more then the Red Baron Ace, he was snoopy! Be

snoopy when it comes to any food for your dog. We **assume** because we are paying more for a dog food, or the store is clean and well-lit, or the proprietor is our good friend, that the food is fresh. Don't assume, be snoopy.

I have been snoopy in Hawaii and found dry dog food manufactured eons ago.

I've also found food with moths and mold sold as premium dog food there. To my knowledge, there are no pet food manufacturers in Hawaii. The length of time for pet food to make it to Hawaii is the reason I would be cautious. A pet store owner in Maui told me that all of her deliveries come in by ship.

If I lived in Hawaii, where **fresh** commercial dog food is hard to find, I would seek out a local, small dog food manufacturer or become an overnight Dog Chef. There is a lot of talk about e-coli in meat and salmonella in chicken, but rarely is the threat of moldy dog food discussed. I have seen cases of pets being very ill and in some cases dying within twelve hours after ingesting dry dog food with mold or canned food with botulism. It happens more often then pet food manufacturers choose to divulge. It boils a chef's blood!

WHAT'S A CHEF TO DO?

If you have chosen to continue with commercial dog food or to use it sporadically (supplementing with fresh food of some kind - right?) - you have many options.

Yogi and I like small pet food manufacturers. There's something about the spirit of the entrepreneur that stirs our stew! Springing up all over the country are small pet food companies. Like micro-brewers, these small companies offer, in many cases, prompt delivery and a new concept - **customer service!** I have had the pleasure of talking with a handful of these folks who are very knowledgeable and helpful about their product **and** pet nutrition.

Often you can get samples to try on your dog, but most of the time you will have to buy a smaller size bag before you know if it's the right food for your particular dog. It may take some time for your dog and his stomach to adjust to these more nutritious and natural diets

being offered in commercial form. The companies range from grain-based companies where you can "just add meat and veggies" to freeze-dried meat products and fermented meat products.

Use my Resource Guide in the back of this book to call some companies. Ask questions, be snoopy; if they are offended thank them for their time and move on.

Because these companies are so small compared to large commercial pet food conglomerates, Dog Chefs like me are left in a paradox. We want these companies to be successful so they will be around for a long time. But, if they become too well-known, will their quality suffer? Will their customer service become as stale as five day leftovers? As Dog Chefs, we learn how to "love 'em and leave 'em" before they leave us.

Yogi has chosen small dog food companies that are closer to our home for delivery and freshness. He eats these foods once or twice a week while we are home and we use them daily while traveling. He likes Monzie's Organics which is an organic muesli for dogs. He especially loves Monzie's cookies. Monzie's is very small, but growing, and is located in Sebastopol, California, not far from our home.

One day delivery away.

Steve's Real Food For Dogs is a freeze dried chicken dinner. They are located in Eugene, Oregon, and offer a great product for traveling or camping with your dog. Grandad's and Feed This, both located in California, sell convenient, prepackaged raw diets for dogs, and ship to your home. (See Resource Guide for further information on all of these products and more.)

To find a small dog food company near you do an Internet Search with key words: specialty dog food companies, pet food companies, gourmet pet food.

In our near future, pet food companies will spring up everywhere, including local meat markets and deli cases. You will have to pay more for **fresh** and/or organic, that's to be expected. Home delivery charges are not cheap. Every Dog Chef will have to weigh the expense with your time and come up with what equals nourishment for you and your dog. Sharing with your neighbors or forming a dog food co-op with friends can cut down on shipping expenses and is good for your soul!

CHAPTER FOUR

THE HUNT FOR MEAT

"Pretend I'm a cow," the butcher said to me, "no, no - pretend I'm a **bullllll-la.**" His voice changed when he "became" a bull. His chest stuck out and his eyes revealed his pride as an imaginary bull. I thought I lost him for good until he came out of his trance and returned to the noisy aisle of the supermarket meat counter.

My new found butcher friend, Victor, loved his job. He was my very first "meat mentor." I was fortunate to find Victor amongst the neatly wrapped meat packets. He sang "O Solo Mio" to his heart's content. People walked by him with a wave or they stopped and were handed a meat packet with a smile and a song. Victor was my man. We were destined to meet, he the teacher, my "wolf-brother," me the student, the pup, ready to learn.

I told Victor I was on the hunt for meat. As a vegetarian, it had been a long time since I hung around the meat counter. I needed a refresher course. There was a loss of spark in Victor's eyes when I told him I was not hunting for meat for myself but for my dogs.

"Your dogs? You mean, woof, woof kind?" he lit up again.

A COW STORY

"Imagine a proud bull like me, yes? I will show you where the major cuts of meat come from using my body as a pretend bull. Now you watch and don't get offended, ok?" Victor didn't wait for my reply but continued in a more scholastic manner.

"Here is my neck, remember it as a chuck roast or pot roast." He picked up two roasts from the meat case to prove his point and put them up to his neck.

"I need my neck to be strong, to protect my family, this part sometimes very tough. But it will be the least expensive."

We moved down to the middle of the meat case where Victor picked up several types of ribs. "Of course you know where these come from on my bull-body. But we have several kinds - baby back ribs, rib steaks, rib roasts and back ribs. Different sizes, tenderness, and, of course, bones." Victor had drawn a crowd and forgot I was his original student asking about meat for dogs. By this time he made suggestions for marinade and sauces for grilling.

"Now, we are at the 'rounds,' tender cuts of meat from the shoulder down." The small crowd was spellbound, watching Victor's hands deftly handle each package that related to his story. His accent added just the right touch of character.

"There are the briskets, cut from behind a cow's front leg or the leg itself. Mostly tough and needing to be cooked a few hours. The flanks are usually cut in strips and used for stir frying. And then we have the loins - oh, **the loins!** " Victor lost a few people in the crowd when he talked about the loins, especially the sir -loins!

I ended my lecture with Victor soon after, but his wonderful pantomime gave me a mental picture I never forgot. When I walked up and down the meat market aisle and found myself in a state of confusion, I pictured Victor, imitating a bull and pointing to his loins! What a great mentor!!

A MEAT MARKET TREASURE HUNT

It's not essential that you get to know a character like my meat mentor, Victor. Most people know meat, and whether you do or not will not deduct points from your Master Dog Chef status.

Red meat will not be the only food you will be serving your dog. There is chicken and turkey and possibly fish. Don't forget the veggies. Whether meat is a mystery, like it was to me, or you're a pro, is not what is important here. Price and what's on sale will factor into your shopping decisions. Also, the size of your dog, how many dogs you have, how new are they at eating fresh and raw foods, their age and health. These are important considerations when deciding your meat choices.

Yogi is two years old and full of piss and vinegar and prone to seizures. He eats his meat raw. I look for meat with more fat, even chicken with the skin and fat.

Hannah is less than ten pounds and is fifteen years old. She's slowing down in life and eats a smaller portion of meat, mostly without the fat.

The meat market treasure hunt is very easy once you learn to focus on your particular dog. Let everything else go that other people have told you. Be open to suggestions from your butcher and most importantly, your dog!

I don't like telling clients exactly what I feed Yogi or suggesting one particular type of meat or the other. I haven't had great success talking with people over the radio or the phone about possible meats for their dog. Lots of people end up with a sister "disease" of **questionitis** called **compar-monia.**

The symptoms of compar-monia can occur without warning. The victim has a conversation or reads a book where someone of some form of credibility suggests to them that this particular meat has been used successfully with this particular dog. Soon, the victim is using that meat for their dog and that meat only. Months later, they feel their dog is no longer getting all of the benefits they possibly could be getting and they see the price of that particular meat skyrocket weekly. That person has full-blown compar-monia! They compared their dog and their life to someone else's, credible or not, and now they suffer. Don't let this happen to you. I will say this until my last day on this Earth as a Master Dog Chef - **YOUR DOG IS UNIQUE AND INDIVIDUAL. YOU WILL HAVE TO LEARN *FROM* HIM WHAT HE CAN AND CANNOT EAT!**

SUPERMARKET SAVVY

You cannot escape the meat market treasure hunt. But here's the good news. I'll give you some great hints and like my friend Victor, my words can follow you through the supermarket aisles.

If you want to get an inside look at your neighborhood grocery store or one of the many large chain stores, use their bathroom. Seriously. Don't fill up your cart, don't buy anything, go to the bathroom.

The good thing about using a store's bathroom is the opportunity to see their back area not visible to the public, especially the large chain stores. Most of them appear clean and spotless. I have been shocked at what I have seen in the back room on my way to the bathroom. It is generally the receiving area for incoming deliveries of food. If it's not clean when you randomly decide to go to the bathroom, when do you think they will be cleaning it? Take your business elsewhere. If you live in a small town and taking your business elsewhere means driving a long distance, then write the store a letter. If you find the situation has not changed then write a letter to the Health Inspector in your county and then take your business elsewhere.

After you've surveyed the bathroom and the delivery area, you're ready then to shop. Supermarkets, even small ones, are laid out for the maximum profit. 50% of those profits come from the edges of the store. That's where the produce, meats, dairy and even salad bars are found. Notice that the milk in the dairy case is always way in the very back. It's such a popular item that by the time you walk clear to the back of the store they are betting on the fact you'll think of something else you need on your return hike to the checkout.

The meat cases are visible from many sides of the store. The one meat case that makes me nervous is the occasional chest freezer found in the center of the aisles. Never buy a chicken or turkey from that case that are stacked over the freezer line. Around Thanksgiving or Christmas is when I have seen this occur the most. These products may have thawed and been refrozen several times without you knowing it. As people come in to buy them the stack gets moved around. The ones that were on the top may have been partially thawed and moved to the bottom and are refrozen. There is no way you can know this. Pay close attention to where and how you buy your frozen poultry.

Another tip to watch out for is ice crystals, whether on meat, dairy products including ice cream. Don't buy the product, the crystals mean that moisture has crept in.

JUST THE FACTS, MA'AM

Here are some quick and easy ideas about meat, poultry and fish that will hopefully haunt you as you're sorting through the meat cases.
- **Don't** be fooled by the wording on meat packages, each supermarket calls its meat something different. They cannot call it USDA Choice unless it really is.
- **Canned** meat products, soups, beef stews, pot pies and packaged frozen dinners, all contain meat of the lowest human consumption. They are leftover bits and pieces and the lowest grade of the

USDA Meat Grading.

- If you find a chuck roast showing the white cartilage near the top of the roast, you have found the first cut, which will be the most tender.
- **This** is a common sense test - if you're not giving your dog a bone, don't pay for it! Buy boneless cuts of meat which appear more expensive, but the amount of meat per pound is less than a cut with a bone. Figure it out!
- If you're using ready-to-eat-hot-dogs as a treat for your dog, cook them first. There is no nutritional value in hot dogs anyway, so cooking will not compromise their use but it will kill the chance of the bacteria, Listeria. If your dog has a weakened immune system, dealing with Listeria is the last thing he needs.
- If you can find "nitrite-free" bacon, you just stepped up one notch as a Dog Chef. Bacon is generally highly nitrated, considered to be table crap in this book.
- **Another** hot dog tale: If they are labeled "all meat" or "all beef" they must contain at least 85% meat or beef. The "all meat" variety can contain a blend of meat. I would also worry about the other 15%!
- If buying lamb, buy New Zealand lamb, since they do not allow the lamb to be hormonized. If you have a choice of leg of lamb, buy the small one for yourself and the larger one for your dog. The larger legs are from older animals, have a stronger flavor, and should be cheaper.
- **Ready**-to-eat-meats contain more fat than fresh meat. More meat by-products can be added, which increases the fat content.
- **The** most commonly purchased meat is hamburger. It provides the most meat fat intake and most of that fat is the saturated type.
- **Ground** meat of any kind has had a large percentage of its surface exposed to the air and light. Grinding also speeds up the loss of vital nutrients. Grind your own meat.
- **Those** marbled, white streaks running through the meat are fat. If the meat is well-marbled, it tells you that the animal was fed a diet high in rich grains such as corn. The fat imparts a flavor to the meat and a level of moisture which helps tenderize the meat. It also says the animal did not exercise a lot.
- **Yellowish** streaks of fat in a steak indicate the cow was grass-fed;

this is a more inferior meat for humans.

- A good hot dog tale: Buy nitrite-free hot dogs without the preservatives or fillers from O.K. Market in Wahoo, Nebraska. I'm not kidding, there is such a place. Call them and see, (402) 443-3015.
- **Buy** ground chuck instead of ground round for hamburger meat; it comes from the area of the animal that is more exercised.
- A free range chicken has an average of 14% fat compared to a standard cooped-up production chicken at 18-20% fat.
- If you think purchasing ground turkey or chicken for fat reduction is best, take yourself down a notch as a Dog Chef. It's the same as lean hamburger.
- The breast meat of wild fowl is always dark because those muscles are used, providing them with a greater blood supply. A production bird rarely uses its breast muscles since it is cooped up all of its life, thus, the large amount of white meat.
- A telltale sign of liquid residue, wet or frozen, on the bottom of a package of meat or poultry means that the food has been previously frozen and the cells have released a percentage of their fluids.
- When buying fish, look for bulging eyes, a shiny look to the skin that springs back when pressure is applied. The scales should look healthy and not falling off or loose, that's the "hair" of a fish, make sure it's not falling out! Gills should be reddish-pink and slime-less. If something smells "fishy," it is. A fishy smell to a fish tells you it has been several days since it was caught.
- The way to really tell if fish is fresh is to place it in cold water. It's fresh if it floats.

MORE FISH STORIES

There are some dogs who live along the coastal areas that were raised on fish.

They have the bacteria in their stomachs to eat fish, raw or cooked. It takes a special Master Dog Chef to know fish and what can be "fishy" about fish. I've often served my dogs **cooked** salmon, but only when it was freshly caught and usually on sale. Unless my dogs were raised on raw fish, they will never experience sushi.

Most of our fish is imported from foreign countries, which have no inspection and have poor sanitary conditions in their processing plants. In the United States we have less than 300 fish inspectors to inspect over 2,100 processing plants and 70,000 fishing vessels.

This information should make you cautious, but should not discourage you from teaching your nose to sniff out bad fish. It's just part of being a chef, especially a Dog Chef.

Yogi's fish intake is seasonal, since we live close to the Pacific coast, the good deals come in with the large catches. When I first gave Yogi fish, I was "poop-detecting" twice a day. I also watched for an increase of itching to make sure he had no skin allergies. He passed all the tests and now eats fish two -three times a month, slightly baked in aluminum foil with garlic and a bit of lemon.

Aquafarming is, and will become, a very big way for a lot of our fish to be raised. Farmed-raised trout, catfish, striped bass, sturgeon and now salmon, are big business items for markets and restaurants. There is still a problem with environmental wastes that need to be worked out, but aquafarming is here for the long run.

If you live in an area where fish are caught within a 100 miles of your local store, then adding fish to your dog's diet might make for good variety.

THE WEIRD STUFF

Most of us can walk down an aisle of a meat market and not shudder when we see the pot roast or the beef ribs. It's the organs that might get to you. Otherwise known as offal, or "awful," as I label it, these are good for most dogs at least one - two times a week. Offal imitates the consumption of the internal organs in the wild. They are the heart, tripe, kidneys and liver. I serve these raw or slightly parboiled by pouring boiling water over this "awful" stuff.

I have never touched a tripe and can't picture myself handling one in the future.

I know several Dog Chefs who feed their dogs raw tripe once a week. It has a tendency to get hard, so don't cook it. Either give it raw or forget it. Each of us Dog Chefs have our hang-ups, this is one of mine.

I buy beef hearts when I can and freeze them, since they generally

are very inexpensive. Yogi likes them but not too often. He knows how to regulate his intake of offal. Beef hearts are generally clean and don't retain toxins. Much better than liver.

I would not suggest feeding your dog too much liver, especially raw. High in Vitamin A, large quantities of liver may present problems. Think prey. If your dog was wild he would possibly be eating liver once or twice a week and that's on the high side.

You may not believe it if you're a beginner Dog Chef, but your dog can learn to self-regulate his food intake, including his knowledge of tipping the balance of his daily and weekly nutritional needs.

If I had a stressful week and had a lapse of memory as to what I gave Yogi nutritionally that week, he will tell me with a look like, "I've had enough of this stuff for a while." Or he'll leave his food. I don't panic, or worry - I remember.

BRINGING IT HOME

You made friends with your local butcher, you enjoyed your hunt for meat, now you have to bring it home and figure out what to do with it. If you're like most Dog Chefs, you'll find that it's a lot more fun hunting for meat than transporting it.

Transporting meat home to your refrigerator takes a lot of common sense, strategy, and occasional rudeness. Surprised? I'm not. I have stood in the hot sun talking to Dog Chef clients of mine who had come out of the grocery store, put their grocery bags of meat in their hot car, and stood and talked with me for 15 minutes or so. All along I wait for them to take notice and say "I've got to scoot, my meat is getting hot."

The proper way to say it is not that your meat "is getting hot," it's spoiling!

WE are one of the best known sources for food contamination. Our own personal transporting of store-bought food and mishandling of meat in the kitchen is as big a problem as transporting meat across the country.

As silly as it sounds, we can be our own worst enemy, or that of our dog, when it comes to "bringing home the bacon."

No matter the weather, your car should be equipped with an ice chest. You know, one of those cheapie styrofoam guys, so if you leave it somewhere alongside the road when you need to change a tire, you don't grieve over the cost.

Ask the grocery bagger to put the cold items together, including the frozen food. (I've had to point out to some baggers that frozen food is considered to be a "cold item.") Take those cold items and put them all in the cooler.

If it's real hot and you had a strategy before you left home, you took along a "blue ice" bag or a milk carton that you filled with water and was now frozen. Or better yet, you go shopping later that evening after the sun goes down.

Let's say you forget your cheapie cooler or Uncle Joe used it as a lawn chair at the last outdoor concert and it's now part of the eco-nightmare. You go shopping and open your trunk to remember the fate of the cooler. Walk your cart full of groceries back into the store, leaving it in plain view of the checkout counter. Walk over to the ice storage and pay 99 cents for a bag of ice. Take your groceries back out to the car, cuss Uncle Joe, and put the cold items (meat, etc.) in the same bag with the ice. **Yes, it is necessary and worth it!**

I have found myself in a similar situation and have bought frozen strawberries in one of those cardboard containers or frozen orange juice and used those to keep things cool. Don't do several other errands after leaving the store. Go home, for tripe's sake!!!

HOME SWEET HOME

As your dog helps you remove the meat from your grocery bags, take a moment to decide the fate of each purchase. I put each meat package in my kitchen sink, that way I will not contaminate my counters and I can thoroughly wash out the sink with hot water. This will give you time to think about your next step.

Look in your refrigerator section and see if you have any meat waiting patiently to be used from a previous buying spree. If not, you can use the following table as a guide for keeping your meat cold or freezing it.

MEATS	DAYS OF REFRIGERATION	MONTHS IN FREEZER
Beef Roasts/Steaks	3 - 5	9
Beef Ground/Stew/Organs	1 - 2	2 - 4
Lamb Roasts/Chops/Ribs	2 - 4	6 - 9
Lamb Ground/ Stew	1 - 2	3 - 4
Lamb Organs	1 - 2	1 - 2
Poultry - All	1 - 2	1 - 2

The above times are just a guide. If you have experienced lengthy power outages, successive days of extreme hot weather or children continually opening and closing the refrigerator doors, or worse yet, not quite closing the door, then these times will vary.

THE AWARD GOES TO...

your refrigerator! Have you thanked your refrigerator lately for all that it has done in the lives of your family and your dog? If not, do it now. If you stop to think about it, you, like all of us, have taken our refrigerator for granted! It's not just an ice cube in disguise. Do you remember the days when it was called the "ice box?" If you do, you're older then me or my memory is shot. The first time I uttered its name, it was called the more refined word, r-e-f-r-i-g-e-r-a-t-o-r.

Refrigeration has been responsible for one of the biggest changes in our lives in the 20th Century. For better or for worse, it has allowed us to store perishable items for long periods of time. It has saved lives with anti-venoms, preserved sperm for future use, made ice for sprains, for our drinks and hangovers. The hum of its motor has kept people awake at night or put them to sleep. It has given us a place for our kitchen magnets where our Dog Chef Shopping List hangs.

Refrigerators also have moved our diets into an evolutionary change - one of frozen foods. Some of those foods are good, a larger percentage are not. For the extra days of freshness we gain from keeping vegetables in the refrigerator, we lose in the increase of consumption of processed food that can be frozen.

For our dogs, the refrigerator is a good thing. Especially as a Dog Chef, we don't have to go hunting daily to catch our dog's food. As good as the refrigerator is to us and our dog's food, it does have **rules**. Adhering to those rules will make your life as a Dog Chef easier and healthier.

Here are some **Refrigerator Rules** for you to live by:

- **Never** refrigerate garlic, onions, shallots, potatoes and tomatoes. They will lose flavor, sprout or turn the starch to sugar.
- **Cool** cooked foods first in the refrigerator before freezing.
- **Don't** freeze foods in aluminum foil. It acts as an insulator and tends to slow down the heat transfer and the food will not freeze as fast as you would want. That leaves it open for bacteria growth.
- A large piece of meat will last longer in the refrigerator compared to smaller cuts or cubed meats or liver. Do not keep without freezing for longer than two - three days.
- **Thaw** meat in the refrigerator, then cook or serve immediately.
- **Never** refreeze meats!
- **Remove** meat from store packaging and rewrap using special products made for freezing if you are planning to freeze longer than two weeks.
- **Raw** poultry and hamburger meat should not be kept in the refrigerator longer than two days without being frozen.
- **To** be safe, change the supermarket wrapping on chicken refrigerated for more than one day. The original wrappings contain blood residue.
- **Fish** can be kept frozen in clean milk cartons full of water.
- **Leftovers** in the refrigerator should be recooked if they've been around for more than thirty-six hours. Especially for meat products, refrigerator temperatures are not cold enough to slow down bacterial growth for any longer period of time.
- **Use** the Zip-Lock bags or comparable products that specifically state they are for freezing. They are less porous and seal airtight.

Rules are meant to be broken. These **Refrigerator Rules** are not written in chicken blood, so you don't have to memorize them. As a Master Dog Chef you do need to strive for the utmost safety and cleanliness that you can muster. You may already be an experienced Dog

Chef and have not had to live by any specific refrigerator rules. Or, you just may have a better refrigerator than Yogi and me. However it works in your house, I hope you will keep in mind the sad statistic that more then one quarter of food poisoning comes from our own negligence at home. Some of us are downright dangerous in the kitchen, and we don't have to be using a knife!

Your dog has a better chance of not being harmed from food poisoning than you do. But making and keeping some concrete kitchen rules for you and your family would make you smarter than the average dog!

KITCHENS RULE, DOGS DROOL!

Your dog is drooling, it's time to take the fresh or thawed meat from the refrigerator and put it in the sink to unwrap it. Before we go any further, a note about thawing is in order. Yogi and I dislike thawing meat in a microwave. In fact, we firmly believe that **real Dog Chefs** don't use microwaves! If microwave manufacturers depended on people like me to consume their product, they would definitely be broke today. I have never owned a microwave and I'm proud of it.

Oh, I know, it's great for heating up coffee or making a baked potato, as so many people tell me why they have one in their house. That's ok, I can live very happily without one.

Also, if you do any cooking for your dog, please don't ever tell me that you do it all in the microwave. I'd have to ask you, **"What's the point?"**

A KITCHEN DESIGNED FOR DOGS

Maybe one day, you'll see an ad in the paper for "kitchens designed for dogs."

You don't have to go that far. But if you have a family or live with one other person, you should consider creating a small space where your dog cooking utensils can all be located. Do you think that's going overboard? Not really. Do it in the name of safety.

Remember, we are becoming Master Dog Chefs, not short order cooks. If you have a corner in your kitchen where "Fredd's" name is plastered everywhere, the other people in the house will know better than to use Fredd's plate or knives or cutting board. You cut raw meat there and use these utensils for that purpose.

Just because you mark the plates, etc., doesn't always mean someone will not use them. My sleepy husband, David, has found himself buttering his toast in the morning on a plate that has "Dogs" written on it. He's not a morning person. It's not always foolproof, but in most cases, it will register with your family after awhile.

I use a permanent marking pen and write across the board and plates and utensils. You have to redo it every few months.

I don't use a cutting board. There is a continuous argument about plastic versus wood cutting boards and which ones are safer. While "they" fight it out, I use a large plate, which works just as well.

Yogi and Hannah get their meat cut for their mouth size and their age. Yogi has larger chunks, up to 2 inches and is an experienced chewer. Hannah has to have her meat cute in small bite sizes. She is very small and much older and chews little and then swallows. Any larger pieces and she can get them caught in her throat.

We all assume that our dogs are good at chewing. They're not. They were born to chew but if they were fed a commercial diet since puppyhood they have to be retrained. Telling that to clients always creates a defensiveness. "My dog can chew, you should see him wolf down his kibble!"

I pop their bubble when I pick up the kibble and break it between my fingers. There is nothing to chew in that crumbly mixture.

If your dog is starting out on fresh meat (raw or cooked) make sure you cut his meat in small pieces. Gradually increase the size of the chunks, so he will need to chew and exercise his gums. This will depend on his chewing ability, his age and if he has teeth or not. Also, does he wolf down his food and regurgitate or does he slow down and chew a few times.

My dog Otis was the only dog I ever had that savored his food. He chewed, looked around at a fly in the air, chewed again, scratched his chest, chewed, sniffed a cat ... he took forever to eat. Dogs don't need to chew their food like we should. They need to chew enough to swallow it safely and to eat slowly enough not to cause bloat. When wolfing down their food, they can take in excess air. If that's the case with your dog, try one of the upright dog table food dishes. They come in many different height and sizes. They may help with excess air intake.

Does your dog chew or not chew, that is the question? It may take you a few weeks to determine that; meanwhile start out with smaller pieces. Even if your dog is large, he may never learn to chew or be able to chew large chunks of meat. Don't force it, you will just have to daily cut his meat.

DID YOU JUST DO WHAT I THOUGHT YOU DID?

Some of us have a kitchen counter or a cutting board that has more germs on it than the area on the rug where your dog scoots across! Gross!

Where do these germs come from if you clean up right away? From your dish rags and sponges! You need to wash these things biweekly in the dishwasher or the wash. Also, give them an early demise. I've seen clients who had dish rags from the World War II era! Give them up!

I much prefer paper towels. Paper towels are necessary in our house with a meat face like Yogi's.

Number two germ spreader is your can opener. Clean it daily. Of course, if you are using only fresh food, you would have very little reason to use a can opener, right?

GERM WARFARE

Germ warfare has become more than a safety issue, it has become a business. A big business!

"Antibacterial - everything" has hit us between the eyes when we walk the supermarket aisles or watch tv commercials. We're scared out of our wits to touch the flusher on a public toilet unless we're armed with a can of Lysol. It's gotten real silly.

Mankind would have totally been wiped off this planet hundreds of years ago if the real culprit of germ warfare was actually a germ lying in wait on the toilet flusher. Todays media make it sound like there are germs waiting to penetrate our un-antibacterial hands. This is one of the better marketing schemes of the 20th Century. Let's leave it behind in the 20th Century and just wash our hands!

Washing our hands before and after preparing food, before eating, after using the bathroom and after changing a dirty diaper will significantly cut down on our chances of "catching something." Using plain old soap will help even more. In a telephone poll conducted for the American Society for Microbiology, 94 percent of Americans said they wash their hands after using a public bathroom. But when the society did some rest-room surveillance, it found only seven out of ten people made the trip to the sink. Women washed more often than men.

Why don't we like to wash our hands? It's the three year old in us. That "inner child" thing still needs to be resolved.

So we're not good at hand washing, what does that have to do with our dogs? Our dogs are well equipped to handle foreign bacteria, their systems are a marvel. Just watch them in your backyard digging up an old bone to chew or eating cow patties or cat turds. Their stomachs can deal with most bacteria, **if they are healthy.**

A chef of any kind washes her hands, whether cooking for her dog or cooking for her family. We don't need to wash our hands in antibacterial crap that actually removes the protective bacteria from our skin and risks bacterial resistance. We just need to **wash our hands!**

The government has reined in the overzealous claims made by marketers of these products. Well-known companies have been fined for making health claims about antibacterial soaps, hand lotion, and sprays. These products possibly have a place in hospitals and for someone who is very ill with an immune problem. I personally don't think they are the answer - anywhere.

LIFE IS SIMPLE GREEN

My favorite choice of cleaning, is Simple Green. You can buy it at any supermarket or hardware store and it is biodegradable and non-toxic. I spray it over my counter, in the sink and on my cutting utensils after handling raw meat. I also use plain white vinegar which has recently been proven to be 99% effective against bacteria, better than bleach and all natural. Bleach is another product that will do the job, but not for me. It's too bleachy. But some of you need chemicals in your life to keep those bogeymen away.

One of these three products are all you need to clean up after your meat cutting. Use hot water and a paper towel and you're set for the next course.

No matter what you use - a cutting board, the counter or a plate, designate that area for **meat cutting only.** Slicing vegetables in the same spot or using the same plate or cutting board, even after you clean up, is not a healthy thing to do. Practice good butchery or the health department fairies will shut down your operation with a bad case of food poisoning.

IF YOU MUST COOK...

Some Dog Chefs will never feel good about giving their dog raw meat, no matter what positive information might come out about it. Or whether they hear that cooking denatures and destroys most of the nutrients found in raw food. Or whether it changes the molecular structure of bones and makes them more brittle and easily breakable when cooked. Still can't serve it raw?

Cooking your dog's food is an unnecessary step in my thinking, but many folks do it regularly and don't mind it. If you feel over-whelmed with home prepared meals for your dog, then you might try to talk yourself into a more raw food diet for "Fredd."

If I haven't convinced you by now with my feelings on not cook-ing food then here are a few good hints on cooking.

Let's start with pans. Aluminum pans are the very worse. As a Dog Chef, I will assume that you know how bad aluminum pans are and get on with it. If you don't know, trust me like your dog trusts you - don't use them.

•Cast Iron or Carbon Steel pans are iron-based and somewhat porous. They need to be seasoned by rubbing with oil and heating them for over a half an hour before first using them. Then, they need to con-tinually be oiled after each washing. Woks are generally carbon steel.

•Teflon and Silverstone have non-stick surfaces as a result of a chemically inert fluorocarbon plastic material being baked on the sur-face of the cookware. These non-stick surfaces allow you to cook with-out the use of fats. With heavy usage and continual cleaning, the coat-ing eventually wears thin and sometimes can come off in the food being prepared. If buying these type of pans, it's best to spend the money for the best.

•Multi-ply Pans are constructed of a layer of aluminum between two layers of stainless steel. Stainless steel is better than an alu-minum pan.

•Enamel cookware is metal coated with a thin layer of enamel. It can chip easily and also can shatter if placed from a very hot range into cold water.

•Glass cookware can cause the glass to crack or break in many inferior brands. Corning ware and Pyrex are the only two recom-mended choices, since both will resist much stress.

•Copper cookware is excellent except for the thin stamped stainless steel pots with a thin copper-coated bottom.

The trick with buying pans is not a trick at all. Never buy cheap! Don't be a pot-scrooge. Buy the best, whether it's for your dog's food or your family's, it's all the same - remember?

WHAT A CROCK!

Crock pots are an economical and time-saving way to cook grains, even for your dog. I would not use it to cook meat. It cooks slowly but also too long and denatures the healthy enzyme action in the meat.

Rice, barley and vegetables all do well in a crock pot. Cooking carrots and broccoli do very little to destroy their nutrients. In fact, cooking opens the cells of these two vegetables enough to release the nutrients and make them more easily digestible and will not cause as much flatulence in your dog's stomach. If you're a Dog Chef with a good nose, that would be a plus!

When cooking grains in a crock pot, wait until the last fifteen or twenty minutes before adding any vegetables. Otherwise, the vegetables **will** become overcooked.

COOKING - IT'S IN YOUR HEAD, YOU KNOW THAT DON'T YOU?

Cooking for your dog is psychological, you know that don't you? Where's your sense of adventure, you're zest for life in its rawest state? Maybe by the end of this book I will break through that psychological barrier of yours and convince you that **"raw is good."** For your dog, and most of the time even for you! Until then, Yogi and I will talk more on cooking.

If you must cook, the simplest and most nutritious way to cook your dog's meat is to put the meat in a saucepan. Cut the meat just enough to fit it in, do not cut it in small pieces first. Put enough **cold** water (keeps the meat tender) in the pot to cover the meat. Put it on the burner and bring it to a boil. Turn off the burner **as soon as it starts to boil.** Remove it from the heat and let it cool down in the pan.

Caution must be taken here that you don't put the pan with the water and meat on the stove and go and do something else - like rearrange your furniture. Be here now! A watched pot does boil, especially with the small amount of water you have in the pot. I am talking from experience here. I have left the room or the house entirely while the meat mixture has boiled over or boiled for a very long time. All of the nutrients and the live enzyme action have disintegrated. The meat ends up being comparable to the leather sole on your shoe. Be here now, hang around, watch your water boil. That's the penance you receive when you decide to cook and not do raw.

There **is** one advantage to **slightly boiling** your dog's food - the excess water and what you can do with it. Whether it is the slightly boiled water from the meat or the vegetables, use it. Pour it over their other food or if you're still serving dried kibble, pour the water over the bowl of kibble. The water from your vegetables is filled with nutrients, make use of that also. Besides pouring it over the rest of the food it can be used in another way.

Buy one or two ice cube trays for your dog and mark his name on the trays. If you have some thick, slightly boiled meat or vegetable water, or a combination of the two, pour it into the ice trays and freeze. Especially in the summer, it will make a wonderful cool treat on a hot day. And the nutrients will help keep your dog in balance and better able to deal with the heat.

Another way to use the water is if you have supplements or cod liver oil that you want or need to add to your dog's food. This is a great cover up, especially chicken broth. Just about anything can be disguised in it.

A slightly boiled chicken soup, with a few slightly cooked vegetables and/or potatoes, is as good for your dog as it is for you. On a cold day or when your dog might seem a bit under the weather, chicken soup for the body and soul works. Yogi has his own recipe in the chapter on YOGI'S RECIPES.

The best way to make a thick chicken soup broth without sacrificing too much of the raw chicken meat by over-boiling, is to take a few pieces of the raw chicken, boil that slightly and then simmer for ten - twenty minutes. Then add the rest of the chicken, heating it for five minutes. That should give you a good stew and broth and take care of your psychological disorder on raw meat at the same time!

EVERYTHING BUT THE KITCHEN SINK

Whether you serve raw food to your dog or you cook his food, the following are some healthy additives or appetizers:

EGGS

The egg is still one of the best and most complete sources of protein. Eggs have been beaten up by the media and the medical establishment because of the high levels of cholesterol found in the egg yolk. But the egg also has a substance called lecithin which is found naturally in eggs and is a factor which may help clear cholesterol. For our dog, three - four eggs a week would be beneficial unless he has a health problem where his body can not control its cholesterol.

Your dog can eat eggs raw and mixed with his raw meat or slightly boiled. Or he can share some scrambled eggs with you on a lazy Sunday morning. One of my clients makes poached eggs for her family and her two dogs. One of her dogs is on daily medication and she has found the poached egg to be a great place to hide the pill.

Boiled eggs are good for long car trips to Aunt Ruth's house. When you stop for lunch, peel the shell, put the egg in a bowl or serve *all dente*, which means you put the whole egg in your dog's mouth!

White or brown eggs are identical in nutritional quality and taste but organic or cage free are best for you and your dog. Showing up in many supermarkets now is a "super" egg called EggsPlus. The hens are being fed a diet high in flax seed, which make them higher in Vitamin E , omega 3 and omega 6 fatty acids. These types of fatty acids have been shown in studies to lower triglyceride levels and increase the good cholesterol HDL. They are a bit more expensive than regular eggs.

Don't ever feed your dog an egg substitute. What's the point and many contain MSG.

How can you tell a bad egg from a good egg? Put your suspect eggs in a bowl of cold water. If your egg goes to the bottom and lies on its side, you've got yourself a good egg. If they start standing up on the bottom they are an okay egg. If they float, forget it, that's definitely a bad egg! Too bad we can't use that method with humans!

The refrigerator life of an egg is around twenty-one days or less. It's best to house your eggs in the original carton for longer life.

BUTTER, YOGURT, MILK, AND CHEESE

Raw unsalted butter is the only recommendation Yogi and I can make for your dog. Yogi eats a large tablespoon of butter with honey two to three times a week to help control his seizures. We don't recommend margarine or butter substitutes. Once again, **what's the point?!** Using margarine or butter substitutes goes against the definition of what is **real food**. Margarine contains 80% fat along with water, milk solids, salt, preservatives, emulsifiers, artificial colors and flavorings. The 80% fat may be tropical oils which are high in saturated fat. What's the point? Real unsalted butter is widely available and should be purchased in small quantities since it will not last as long as salted butter.

Yogurt is good on a daily basis or a few times a week or whenever you might be eating some. Plain yogurt is all a Dog Chef would serve. You don't need to get fancy with the flavored kind or the "fruit on the bottom" choices. They contain lots of sugar.

Plain yogurt can help your dog with diarrhea or gas or an upset stomach. Try a small dollop to see if your dog likes it.

Many people ask me about cow's milk for their dog? It certainly depends on the dog and where and how he was raised. Cow's milk is not recommended for most dogs, but before condemning it further, I do know of several dogs that were raised on or near dairy farms. They were fed cow's milk soon after birth and grew up drinking cow's milk and eating a raw meat diet. They appear perfectly healthy.

Soy or rice milk is more pleasing to a dog's stomach, but there again you have to use it cautiously to see what reaction it has a few hours later. Let your dog finish your soy or rice milk after you've eaten your cereal. Then follow him around for a day.

Goat's milk is given quite often in place of cow's milk and many dogs raised with milking goats drink it daily.

Cheese is another questionable additive, like cow's milk. Many of the dogs we have today originated in parts of the world where cheese was a very big part of their diet. It doesn't exactly mean that your dog should and would do well eating cheese. Yogi and I would keep cheese as a treat, if it agreed with your dog's insides.

Cottage cheese is used by many home cooking advocates to add to their dog's diet. Cottage cheese is a high-moisture soft cheese and will loosen your dog's bowel movements after a period of time. Keep that in mind when using it.

Cheeses come in soft all the way to very hard. That tells you as a Dog Chef that the soft cheeses have a high-moisture content and the firm to very hard cheeses are very low in moisture. If you're feeding your dog hard cheeses under the table and he consistently has constipation, forget the cheese for awhile.

Dogs on medication should not be fed cheese. Cheese is made from a bacterial culture or specific mold cultures. They sometimes interfere with medication. Cheese has a high salt content, with the very hard cheeses having the highest salt content.

ARE YOU NUTS?

In small quantities, nuts are a healthy staple for your dog, although, Yogi and I do not include peanuts. We don't consider peanuts a healthy choice for friend or foe. A very large percentage of dogs has an allergy toward peanuts, along with their human counterparts. There are many other nuts in the sea, try those out.

Sunflower seeds are used quite often in healthy dog diets. Some people take sunflower seeds and other nuts, grind them in their blender and put them in with their dog's raw or close to raw meat.

Yogi likes a "nut butter" I make with ground up nuts stirred with unsalted butter and honey.

A BIT OF TUSCANY

One of my clients has a dog she found in Italy while living there for two years.

It's part Doberman and something else. The dog's name is Covina and she loves pasta.

Covina eats pasta with three tablespoons of extra virgin olive oil, blended raw vegetables and raw meat. Covina was raised on pasta and thrives on it. If your dog likes pasta, use it one or two times a week along with his protein dish.

Garlic always sounds good with a pasta dish, so we'll sneak it in here. When God made dogs, it was on the same day that garlic was created! What a wonderful, stupendous, terrifically-potent, incredible idea garlic was! Thanks God!

All of the money spent on pharmaceuticals and vitamins and anti-bacterial sprays and lotions to supposedly keep the bogeyman away can simply be taken care of with raw (here's that word again; **raw!**) garlic. Notice I didn't say garlic tablets, I said garlic. There are a few oral products on the market for us humans to take that will allow us to still have a social life after consuming garlic. For our dogs' breath, give him parsley. That's good along with his raw garlic.

As usual, start out slowly. Cut a garlic clove in half and daily give that to your dog in his food. Be clever and hide it somewhere if he doesn't like it. Work your way into a clove daily or more if he can tolerate it. Remember, when cutting the clove, you don't need to peel every speck of the garlic paper off of the clove, you're dog won't mind. Try this - put the clove on a hard surface, hit the clove with your fist, then remove the paper. It will come off easier.

As a Dog Chef, you will need to get close to garlic. It's only natural. When you finish this book, your assignment is to read more about garlic. Garlic is that "staff of life" everyone's always talking about, it's just that bread stepped in and took the credit. Embrace garlic for you and your dog like a long lost friend. Get reacquainted, get close. I guarantee that you will forget your veterinarian's phone number after months of daily serving garlic. You won't be calling him very often.

Since we're on the subject of pasta and garlic, it's appropriate to talk about oil, not the kind that comes up out of the ground but the kind that grows on trees. Olive oil. Since you're probably using a lot of olive oil for yourself, how about adding a teaspoon or more to your dog's food on a daily basis? Buy a good brand in your grocery store or check the resource guide in the back of the book for quality sources.

Every Chef has to splurge on one food, paying a bit more for the quality. Since Yogi and I live in the Napa Valley of California, we have an incredible variety of olive oil at our paws. This is where we splurge. We buy olive oil from several local sources, one being the St. Helena Olive Oil Co. (see Resource guide). They create a Lemon Olive Oil that we use for everything.

A SWEET TREAT

Here I go again, but I'm **assuming** that you know better than to feed your dog chocolate. And that you have also informed your kiddies about the dangers of feeding him chocolate?

There is one sweet that Yogi and I like and that is honey. Of course, we are using our common sense and only giving it to our pals two to three times a week if they are healthy. With all of that out of the way, we can digest what a unique sugar honey is. It is so unique that it will not grow bacteria! Think about that for a minute and consider what a marvel that is in this world! Wow! It is also twice as sweet as granulated sugar! Another Wow! Think about **that** for a moment. We humans work to granulate sugar through a long process. We have to have a building to do this in and hire people and form unions and pay truckers to haul it and we have to package it and sell it. Then a little bee comes along and hits a few flowers and drinks some nectar on his way home. His little body stores the nectar, until he gets to his hive. In a sac just above his intestine where enzymes are secreted, the starch is broken down into simple sugars and fructose. He pumps the nectar mixture in and out of his body until the carbohydrate concentrate is about 50 - 60% and then deposits it into the honeycomb. That's a simple version of a remarkable story of a **real food** - honey!

Yogi and I have had countless discussions with people of the veterinarian persuasion who condemn honey, like many other real foods, for dogs. You might be surprised to hear that I agree with them **IF** the dog is on a commercial dog food diet! Then he is getting too much sugar of any kind.

The best and only type of honey Yogi and I dine with is the "unheated" kind. This is the highest quality of honey and is not nutrient-depleted by the heat processing. "Unheated" is the key word here. Not "uncooked" or "raw." Honeys that are labeled "unheated" can not be heated over beehive temperature on a hot day - that's 100 degrees Fahrenheit. 80 - 90% of unheated honey turns into enzymes for digestion, assimilation and utilization. Honeys that are labeled "raw" or "uncooked" can be heated up to 160 degrees, which is done to thin the honey for quicker filtering and easier bottling. These honeys turn into radical blood sugar.

For Yogi, his honey and butter treats help with his seizures. The "unheated" honey combined with the "certified raw unsalted" butter balances his body when it shorts out. Do not use a substitute for either type of honey or butter we recommend. They must match that criteria, otherwise they are not **real food,** but man made and all of the buzzing around that poor little bee went through is for naught!

YOU DIRTY VEGETABLE!

If someone called you a vegetable, take it as a compliment! Webster's dictionary describes a vegetable as "animating, hence, full of life." It's hard to believe when we see a carrot or a celery stick lying on the counter that it would be "animating and full of life," but it is. It's brimming over with life!

What vegetables would be good for your dog? Try them out, interview them, see what happens a day later when you change your Dog Chef hat to a Poop Detective hat. Watch with bated breath what the "end" result is.

Unless your dog is already "veggie savvy," my suggestion would be to start with the basic carrot and go from there. One is good to start. Steam it for a minute or two **only!** Then slice and serve with the other food.

Another way, is to take a raw carrot and stick it in your blender and blend it until it is fine. Mix that with your broth or your raw food. That way, it is easier to digest.

One more way is to juice a carrot, if your dog is sick or can't digest it well. Pour the juice in with your broth and mix with the rest of the food. You can do this with broccoli and most other vegetables also.

Don't get carried away with vegetables and try to serve them all. I have had some clients try to make up for their sins of not eating very many vegetables by giving their dog several different kinds. Sorry, it doesn't work that way. If your dog sleeps in the bedroom with you, you'll be opening the window in the middle of the night and possibly doing a "night run" to satisfy his loose bowels.

Keep it simple and serve it slowly. Then settle on a few seasonal and regional veggies for your dog and yourself. The saying, "The fruit does not fall far from the tree" are words of wisdom. Here in California, our choices are many when it comes to vegetables and fruit. Anytime of the year, all year round. As Dog Chefs, we need to keep it in perspective. To our dog's ancestors, a rabbit was a rabbit, not a gourmet specialty.

YOU CRAZY FRUIT!

If you were to say to your dog, "Come here, my little fruit." You would, once again according to Webster, be saying, "Come here, my little *enjoyment!*" That's what a fruit is - enjoyment! Along with the great vitamins, minerals and stuff, eating a fruit is as pleasurable as living with our dogs!

Bananas, apples, prunes, grapes and even watermelon can be great food for our dogs - even enjoyment. Keep it simple and serve it slowly.

Yogi and I would suggest giving your dog the fruit mixture in the morning and the veggie mixture in the evening. That will keep the gas in your dog's stomach to a minimum. Fruit and veggies don't mix well, even in humans.

BLEND IT ALL TOGETHER

If there was a fire in my house, I've instructed Yogi to grab the blender. I have a Vita Mix Blender and it's priceless! It is so powerful, we use it to mow our weeds in the springtime!

Blenders and juicers are as important to a Dog Chef as dog treats are to dogs.

You may not feel the need for something of the quality of a Vita Mix but down the road you might.

Yogi and I take chicken backs, necks and sometimes whole carcasses (split up) with some water. Turn on the blender and a minute later we have "chicken pate!" We freeze it in small portions and when on the road we mix with kibble or muesli. No fuss, no hassle. And the bones are blended fine, easily digestible and adding minerals to the diet.

If you had to choose between your blender or your microwave, I would hope you would choose the blender without a bit of hesitation. Real Dog Chefs love blenders!

RAW, RAW, RAW!

After a few months of creating home prepared meals for your dog, Yogi and I hope that when someone ask you what you give your dog for food that your cheer will be "Raw, raw, raw! Otherwise, **what's the point?"**

CHAPTER FIVE

NOT ALL DOGS EAT ALIKE

Let's pretend that you're hosting a small dinner party tonight. The five people attending the informal affair are: your Uncle Harry (who is a diabetic and suffers from gastritis), your younger sister Sally (who is pregnant), Sally's mischievous four year old son, your mother (who has an acid reflux condition and is quite obese), and last but not least, your next door neighbor, Ralph, who will only be joining you for dessert (since his hemorrhoids are acting up!) What will you serve for dinner? As the chef for the evening, you will have to sit down and determine many things about your choice of food.

As a Dog Chef you must do the same, and as you live with different dogs, you will find it is similar to hosting a dinner party for a few of your dog's friends. The same considerations will have to be paramount.

When talking to people about their dog, the conversation tends to come back to what their dog does and doesn't eat, as well as how well they eat it or what physical condition prevents them from eating specific food. As with humans, we focus on our dog's condition. We are aware of what food makes our dog sick, uncomfortable, or gives him gas.

Unlike humans, a dog's digestion takes place in a few hours. Thus, in a short period of time, the votes are tabulated and the results are in. What, or how much Fredd ate a few hours ago will either come back to haunt us or not be heard from again. This is probably one of the first things we learn about our dogs when they initially come into our home.

I've never had a conversation with someone about their dog without hearing how finicky their dog is, that their dog will eat anything, or what happens when they eat this or that. We know this stuff about our dogs. Why then do we have so many questions?

If you invite Uncle Harry, who is a diabetic and suffers from gastritis, over for dinner, you're probably not going to serve cheese fondue. You're probably not going to serve your pregnant sister Sally a vertical tasting of five different Cabernet wines, or offer her four year old son raw oysters. Your common sense clicks in and you save those food experiences for the right people who will enjoy them. Your dog is no different. As a puppy you are going to feed him for growth. If your dog is pregnant, you will feed her and her soon to be newborns. And when your dog becomes a senior, you will feed him with fewer calories. And for each stage, you will feed them for **nourishment**.

Preparing meals at home for your dog means you will need to pay attention to his ever changing body. That's really no different than primarily feeding a dog with commercial dog food, or at least it shouldn't be. It's nothing to obsess about anymore than you do for your own diet.

HOW DO YOU KNOW THIS STUFF?

Master Dog Chefs have three extraordinary qualities that separate them from the pack. The first is their use of an inherent ability that every human is born with and every dog possesses. That ability is called **common sense.** Plain and simple common sense. The more folksy or simple our common sense, the better we can relate with our dog.

The ultimate degree Yogi and I feel someone should be studying

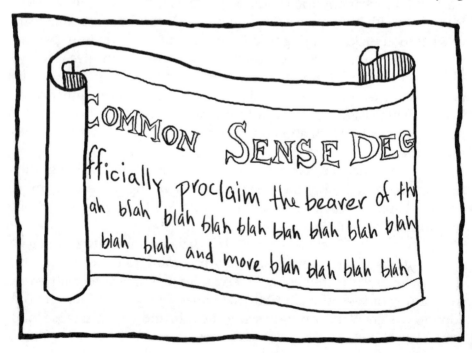

for is the one we have after our names on the cover of this book - **C.S.D. : Common Sense Degree.** You are living right if you have a C.S.D. behind your name!

As a client of mine asked recently, "Where do I get one of them there Common Sense Degrees?" The answer: you bestow it upon yourself when you feel you are worthy (or when you finish reading this book you can tear out the back form and send it to our Dog Chefs of America™ address and we will grant you a C.S.D).

Common sense comes from dumbing down our intellect, quieting the mind from nagging questions, from listening to far too many experts, and getting in touch with that special gift we all possess called intuition. **Exercising quiet** is the second quality that separates a Master Dog Chef from a short order cook. When the confusion of worry and doubt enters our mind on what might be healthy for our dog and whether we are feeding him everything he needs, we must walk away, change our focus and then take action. Cook something, sharpen our knives, cut up some meat, hum a tune. Make room for common sense. It's there, under the worry and doubt.

The third quality of a Master Dog Chef is: **when in doubt, do nothing!**

Another way to say it is when in doubt, do less. If you've read a few books on cooking for your dog and the daily list of ingredients has become longer than your arm, check off a few of the ingredients and use only those. In a matter of weeks try some of the others. Less is always best.

Some of the best chefs for humans are the ones who make good use of quality food but keep the serving simple. Remember that with your dog.

COMMON SENSE AND CRUD WITHIN

If you take your common sense and consider why humans and animals have lived for so long without being wiped off the planet by some bacterial bogeyman, you might come up with an interesting theory. Our version is what we call the **crud-theory**. All of us, whether human or animal, have been able to live amongst the bacteria around us because of the crud within us!

Think about that for a moment - there's crud around us and crud within us! Perhaps not a good thought, but it's true. And it keeps us alive! Our dogs are further blessed, that's why they can spend countless hours licking their butt and not getting sick, or showing up after a short absence with a "necklace" of deer crap. We catch them eating a cow paddy and savoring it. Does it help to know that adorning themselves with the smell of the wild while eating the wild goes back to their days of living in the wild?

Our domesticated dogs still have "wild" in them. We can dress them in little coats to keep them warm and allow them to share our bed, but somewhere inside of us, we envy them. Yogi and I like to think that it is because of their latent wild state. The uninhibited beings that they are represent a state where our rational thinking and intelligence won't permit us to go. But we love to watch!

Most of us prefer that our dogs smell good to our senses, not theirs, so we perfume their bodies and shampoo their treasured deer-crap necklaces. We can be forgiven for our desire to live with our somewhat domesticated pets in an environment that smells good to us. But as Master Dog Chefs, we must keep in mind that some dogs will need more "wild" in their lives than other dogs. If they can't get it by rubbing themselves in some form of animal waste then we must provide it for them in food form.

I have a client named Rose who has a Cattle Dog mix called Ringo. Ringo had a moth-eaten appearance to his fur and was quite sickly. Rose took Ringo to the vet where blood tests were given and he was put on a special canned food diet. Months later, Ringo got worse and his blood tests revealed nothing. Soon after, Rose started feeding Ringo raw food, after reading up on home prepared meals for dogs. When Rose called me, Ringo had vastly improved, but Rose was concerned that when she fed Ringo on the backyard deck she would see him drag his meat through the dirt in the yard. Or he buried it and fifteen minutes later dug it up again and then ate it.

Rose started feeding Ringo in the house to keep him from his odd behavior with his food, but he refused to eat while in the house.

"Why are you changing his feeding location?" I asked.

"Because it's dirty!" Rose replied.

"He's a dog and he doesn't think it's dirty, it's seasoning!" I chimed.

As a Master Dog Chef we must realize that seasoning doesn't just come from a little can in our spice rack. To a dog, everyone's backyard is filled with a cornucopia of Mother Nature's best!

A year later, Ringo is still dining outdoors and thriving on his self-seasoned cuisine.

For humans and dogs, a diet kept the same or too clean, will not allow our bodies to equip themselves with the bacterial defenses they need when encountering the dreaded bacteria bogeymen we some-times come in contact with through food or water.

Dogs have a natural ability to withstand crud of some of the worst proportions. A dog is a natural born crud eater. The less man-made the crud, the better. It's not our job to find crud for our dog to eat. They do a good enough job themselves, thank you. Our task is to feed our dog the closest thing possible to a raw state and still be able to deliver the goods.

One quick note here for you super-clean freaks, if you drop a piece of meat on your floor while preparing it for your dog, don't throw it away! Your dog will eat it, you're not cooking for a cat! If you just can't stand it, wash the piece and give it to your dog. If he is eat-ing outside, he will be doing worse. Don't waste it!

Julia Child, the well known chef for humans, has a thirty second rule for food that is dropped on the floor. She believes you can still eat it if it spends less than thirty seconds on the floor. As Master Dog Chefs, Yogi and I believe in the thirty <u>minute</u> rule. If you drop a piece of your dogs' food on the floor and you are busy doing something else or you didn't see it until you started cleaning up, than use the the thir-ty minute rule!

There are dogs that can live very healthily on canned food and kibble. Other dogs need supplementation of their diet and others need whole, natural home prepared meals. As our dogs age, move into motherhood, or they exercise more or less than before, we must be vig-ilant and compensate for those changes.

Even when our status at home changes, such as taking a full time job when we previously worked at home and thus having to leave our dog alone for longer hours, this will also mean changing his diet. Or a change of who is or is not living in the house any longer due to a death, divorce or children going off to school.

Many ongoing studies on the feelings of animals have shown the effect that changes have on them, physically and behaviorally. During changes in our lives, we must consider how the experience is effecting our dog's life and pay closer attention to his food intake.

IT'S ALWAYS HARD TO CHANGE

Change is difficult for us humans. For that matter, it's even harder for many dogs. But we know just by looking in the mirror or at some old photos of us and our dog that, like it or not, change is definitely taking place!

The hardest trick of being a Master Dog Chef is learning to deal with continuous change. We must be able to let go of what was working great for us and our dog and move into foreign territory at the drop of a chefs hat.

Let's say you take that million dollar offer on a job that will give you more exposure to the world but less time spent on your home turf. Your family will be around to help out but that means Fredd will not be fed at the same time each day until things get worked out and Fredd will not be exercised as consistently as before. Home prepared meals are still going to be served to Fredd but now they need to be tailored for easier handling by whomever is elected to feed Fredd. With the help of some of the folks we have listed in our Resource Guide, Fredd should continue to be well-fed.

When the time comes when you and your family adjust to the new household schedule, Fredd's diet needs another overhaul. Fredd also needs to be looked at from head to toe. How does Fredd look? What does his fur look like? How has he been acting? How's Fredds' poop? Then ask Fredd how Fredd is doing? Ask yourself how you (and your family) and Fredd are getting along?

These close encounters should optimally take place once a month, two at the most. Scheduling Fredd in your busy calendar is more important than your hair appointment and it will help you feel like you are more in control of your life.

Physical changes in our dogs can take a few years but also can appear to happen overnight. We need to do a monthly inventory on the pets that we are feeding, no matter how busy we are. We are the big kahunas, the place where the buck stops - we are the Master Dog Chefs. That means, **we are in charge!** Our vet is not in charge, nor is our pet sitter, it's us. It's up to us, as Master Dog Chefs, to know how our "restaurant" (our dog) is doing each month, and take inventory.

This may appear overwhelming to you, but appearances are deceiving. Yogi and I have a wonderful way for you to stay on track with your dog and not get stressed. We have two **Master Dog Chef Rules** for you to write down and keep in front of you at all times. These rules will help you stay focused and remove the chatter from your own head and from the mouths of others.

MASTER DOG CHEF RULES

1. ALWAYS BE WILLING TO CHANGE.

2. NOURISHMENT IS THE MOST IMPORTANT INGRE-DIENT.

Not bad rules, eh? Let's talk about each rule and see how easy this all can be.

1. Always be willing to change. Earlier, we talked a bit about change and how it might effect your dog and his diet. From puppy-hood to his senior years, your dog's body will go through many changes. The food you feed him and the amount will vary with those changes. Factor in your lifespan with your dog to consider making a dietary change of some sort every two to three years. It may not be a major change, but possibly some slight adjustments here and there.

Do you remember the days when you lived on pizza and beer? Or ice cream and potato chips? Or sugar-coated cereal? Not exactly Master Chef material, but hopefully your mother balanced your diet with better food. As you aged, your food choices became more discriminating.

If we raise our dogs from puppyhood, we know that they are growing "kids" with big appetites and will have an occasional "fling" with their version of pizza and beer. Soon after their second year, they will need their food evaluated once again, with considerations of how well their bodies are adjusting to the demands of being a teenager along with their behavior. Contemplating some sort of dietary change every two years is a good measuring stick.

A JOURNAL IS GOOD

If you have children, you may have had some way of watching them grow, either with a measuring stick on the wall or with a photo album. It's not insane to keep a journal of your dog, even if you did not get him as a puppy. All great Master Dog Chefs do it. It's the best way to keep track of your dog's health, his growth, and his diet.

Writing in a journal about our dog is not silly, it's smart. Years ago when I flew as a flight attendant with an overseas airline, I had a wonderful experience of finding myself in an antique store in Japan, outside of Tokyo. I came across an old tattered leather journal. The cover was my attraction. There was a black and white photo of a medium-sized dog pasted on the front cover. He stared into the camera and appeared to be smiling. Thumbing through the delicate paper were drawings of the dog in different environments. One was of him pulling a cart, another herding other animals.

The journal was written in Japanese, but most of the drawings of the dog were self-explanatory. One drawing relayed an experience of the dog being in some sort of accident where his back leg was severely cut. Pools of blood were drawn around the dog's leg as he lay on the ground. There were several paragraphs of writing next to the picture and I then came across a lined insert of pictures of plants and herbs that had been used to care for the injured dog. I recognized the ginger plant and the hot pepper plant, which had an "=" sign next to them showing another picture of the plants in grated form. The following picture showed a hand applying the cayenne-type mixture onto the wound to stop the bleeding (since that discovery, I have used ground cayenne pepper to stop bleeding in many animals and humans, including myself).

The Japanese shopkeeper could speak broken English. I asked her how common it was for a Japanese to keep such an extensive journal on an animal.

"All time for farmers," she said, showing me the farmer's name and his emblem.

"Farmers always keep journals for best animals in case farmer die, no problem."

Not buying that journal is on my short list of regrets. What a treasure trove of information, respect and compassion about the relationship between a farmer and his dog.

Keeping a journal on your dog allows you to make dietary changes without the usual fanfare that might normally accompany your decision. Your dog's journal shows his growth in spurts, reveals his weakest physical conditions, and tells you volumes about him in general. It also is there for your dog and whomever might have to assume responsibility for him if you leave this world for the Great Kitchen in the sky. Like the Japanese shopkeeper said to me about the Japanese farmer, "Farmers always keep journals for best animals in case farmer die, **no problem!**"

2. Nourishment is the most important ingredient. All of the anxiety that seems to come from feeding our dogs non-commercial food can be alleviated if we focus on one ingredient - **nourishment.**

You may recall from the Introduction in this book, that Websters definition of **to nourish** is as follows:

1. to feed and cause to grow, to supply with matter necessary to life and growth. 2. to support. 3. to supply the means of support and increase to; to encourage; as, to nourish rebellion. 4. to cherish, to comfort. 5. to educate; to instruct. And to use **common sense** as Yogi and I have added.

I talked with a client a few months ago who read to me a list of ingredients that made up her dog's newly prepared meals. The list was long.

"Do you feed your dog each one of those ingredients every day? I asked.

"Yes," she replied.

"You never miss a day in your busy schedule?"

"No," she answered.

"You must thrive on discipline." I said in astonishment.

"No, I know that if I don't do it, Casey will be undernourished and get sick," she said.

There it was, the other side of the coin. The dog chef who is bewildered by the definition of nourishment and over-feeds her dog. She had been successful with the first part of the definition by feeding her dog, which caused him to grow. Where she had become obsessive and confused was the second half - **to supply with matter necessary to life and growth.** For our dogs, supplying the matter necessary to life and growth does not mean relentlessly feeding the same stuff every day without paying attention to whether our dog needs it that day or not. That leads to overfeeding and ignorance of the natural process of our dog's body. In fact overfeeding is worse than underfeeding a dog!

FOOD, TOO MUCH FOOD

When a dog is overfed or can eat throughout the day at his whim, we have removed his purpose and a time for special attention. We have also messed with his sense of survival. Overfeeding a dog weakens that important natural instinct that his body is equipped with - the will to fight and live. A dog whose body is continuously in digestive action can never rest. If a little food is good, more is <u>not</u> better. Our obsession with overfeeding and our over concern with food in general, can actually interfere with good health.

Domestication has made food addicts of some of our pets. As a Dog Chef, understanding that overfeeding is not nourishing or is not a sign of love, is a quantum leap towards the achievement of a **COMMON SENSE DEGREE**. In the wild, your dog would go for several days without eating anything.

Food is nourishing when it is used by the cells of the body and does not have to be continuously stored. An occasional fast for your dog is healthy, if he is healthy. If he's not healthy, you might notice that his body will make him fast in its own way. He will eat less than normal or not eat at all. The word goes out to all of the organs to shut the engines down and give 'em some rest.

Fasting a dog one day a week or at least two days a month helps their digestive tract and allows their system to rest. Many people who do home prepared meals for their dog factor in a weekly or twice monthly fast into their feeding program. Some people do the cold turkey approach and pick a day each week and just make water available for their dog and the continual attention that comes with cooking and preparing meals each day. You don't want your dog to think he did something wrong. Pat him on the head, give him a short massage, and tell him you are doing this for him and the next day his food will taste wonderful.

Some people I know make the fasting day a time for bone chewing. No other food is offered, just raw bones. You can read much about bones in the book titled GIVE YOUR DOG A BONE by Ian Billinghurst.

Yogi does not fast for a whole day because of his seizures. He has a low blood sugar problem. But we do pick one day a week when his spirit is at its best and skip the evening meal.

Fasting your dog allows you to understand his body even better. I know several people who fast their dogs for one day weekly and do the same for themselves. It's a family thing and they love it!

If your dog is not healthy, you will need to read more about fasting, or if your vet has a good understanding of it and its powers, consult with him or her.

HEALTHY   OVERWEIGHT   OBESE

THE OTHER SIDE

It's more common for people to overfeed their dogs than to underfeed them. But I have had clients who did just that because they were not observing their dog's energy level, they thought their dog should eat less, or they were not feeding their dog nourishing food. Or they just wanted to save money.

None of these underfeeding excuses will ever elevate a short order cook to Master Dog Chef status!

Below is a picture from Yogi that shows you how to look at your dog's body and see if you're overfeeding or underfeeding him.

ALWAYS EATING, ALWAYS HUNGRY

A dog that is ravenously hungry all the time and eats constantly, is a dog that is starving from a lack of nutrients. Most of the time, these dogs are thin and look under-fed. Home prepared meals of real food, especially the kind that allows the dog to chew will take care of his hunger.

Chewing creates a very important digestive aid that will help the dog digest his food better. Gradually adding raw bones that have large chunks of meat on them will make the dog chew and wrestle to get his food off of the bone and accelerate enzyme action. A constant craving for food should inspire your Dog Chef imagination to find **real food** that is more fresh and wholesome, such as raw meat and bones, grated carrots, apples, and oatmeal with a small amount of honey added to the water.

CHUBBY CANINES

Your dog eats by your hand, not his paw. Chubby or obese dogs are usually an indication of an overzealous short order cook with a misconception of **real food** and good nutrition. We have yet to discover the dog who gets up in the morning and prepares eggs, bacon and buttered toast for himself or a chicken fried steak for dinner.

The chubby canine's short order cook needs to elevate themselves to a higher level if the dog is fat because of overfeeding or feeding poor quality food. Feeding the wrong food to a dog can result in obesity simply because that food may contain more calories per serving than a dog needs to maintain its ideal body weight.

Generally, we've found the short order cooks who have overweight dogs are feeding the dog the same food or menu they were feeding them when they were puppies. Hello! Change is hard, but change you must!

DON'T FORGET SNACKS

I had a client who, in her own defense, read to me exactly what she fed her fat nine year old dog, Pia, each day. If I had been talking to her on the telephone, I would have been in a quandary as to the reason why Pia was so overweight. Her menu sounded healthy.

Since I was standing in their living room, I was able to read between the lines and see the true dining experience that went on daily for the dog. Throughout the living space were small bowls of peanuts, candy, cookies and crackers. Snacks were the basis of food consumption in this house. Pia was just joining the pack!

Being a dog small enough to jump from chair to chair, she left enough snacks on each plate to keep her humans from being suspicious. It was difficult to see how anyone would not catch on to Pia's capers, since her bed hid the evidence. Cookie crumbs were scattered throughout her blankets.

There was a lack of observing Pia and her behavior in this household, especially since it didn't take a detective to figure out how the dog was consuming extra calories with the snack bowls conveniently located in every nook and cranny.

To be a Master Dog Chef, one does not have to be Sherlock Holmes. The simplest answer is usually the right solution, we just have to be more observant. Pia was just joining the pack and doing what the pack did nightly - snack. More than likely the word was out to the family not to feed the dog any snacks because she was on a diet. Not understanding such human logic, Pia did what any healthy pack animal would do, she made herself at home with snacks, even if it meant eating alone.

To confirm Pia's behavior, we ate from the snack bowls for a few minutes while Pia begged. We left the room shortly after, leaving Pia in the house by herself while we observed her from an outside window. Less than a minute later, Pia jumped up on one of the chairs and ate three cookies from the plate.

There was nothing sneaky about Pia's behavior. The snack bowls were in eye level of a three year old and this was the family's way of bonding through food. Pia was being part of the family. Pia's family did not see such an obvious problem because they considered snacks to be snacks, not a part of the bigger meals. Food is calories, no matter whether we call it breakfast, lunch, or snacks.

The change for Pia came with a change of snacks. Snack bowls were traditionally left in their places but the type of snacks changed. Not for the family, they still ate their cookies and candy, but they brought those snacks in the room, when they were there. The snack bowls were now filled with small baby carrot sticks, popcorn and rice cakes with a small dab of nut butter. Pia still tested the bowls on a daily basis, but the carrot sticks became more of her toys than her food, and she lost the five pounds she needed to lose.

Snacks are the downfall of many chubby canines. Remember what your mother used to yell to you before dinner, *"Don't eat too many of those snacks or you'll ruin your dinner!"*

Master Dog Chefs don't look too kindly on snacks. Most dog snacks, or treats are table crap and that's not good food for thought!

MORE TREATS

It's a pity to see Dog Chefs work so hard to maintain their dog's diet and then destroy it with treats that are just plain food crap. It would be better if they walked over to a field of cows, picked up a cow paddy and gave that to their dog. At least it would be real!

If we think prey, very few treats of today factor into that equation. Many years before the advent of commercial dog food as we know it, treats were real food of some sort. An apple, popcorn, meat chunks or bones. Real Bones! Not the compressed version, or the sterilized ones, or the smoked ones, or the rawhide ones. These were real, bloody bones.

Then came the misguided idea that real bones were bad for dogs and a billion- dollar chew stick market was born. Straight out of a Forrest Gump movie, we can find rawhide chews, and jerky-flavored chews, and peanut-butter chews, and pig hooves, donkey hooves, lamb ears and even pig penis. There are also plastic and rubber bones and bones made from petrochemicals, some of which are held together by a cousin to Elmer's Glue.

We know that dogs love treats and that their owners love to give dogs treats, but what's in the treat? If it's a dog cookie, read the label. If it includes ingredients that don't sound like something from your kitchen, than put it back on the shelf. Look for homemade treats (many people sell them locally), or contact one of the resources we have listed for Ready Made Food. Monzie's Originals makes great dog cookies along with many other resources.

For chew sticks, not much can be recommended except the few we have listed in the Resource Guide. Rawhide chews can give your dog endless hours of chewing, but also create havoc in their intestines or promote choking. Ask your vet, they can tell you horror stories of chew toys.

If we look at the array of chew toys available for dogs, they all have one thing in common: they are made with humans in mind. They appeal to our sense of cleanliness and are bleached and sterilized so the chew does not soil the rug. They are manufactured in colors that "just make us want to chew them ourselves," as one friend told me. They glow in the dark (what's that all about?), or they are made from plastic and are "not designed to be consumed," as we can read on some labels. Why do they add chicken flavoring to the plastic bone if dog's aren't supposed to eat or chew it? We're confused.

Keep in mind, there are no regulatory standards on treats and chew bones, especially the rawhide and animal hooves, etc. Those can come from other countries where standards for the use of toxins is nonexistent. As a Dog Chef, you need not be concerned because you will throw out all of your non-real food items and get serious. It's time for you to supervise your dog when he's chewing and give your dog a real raw bone!

THE CANINE GAS CRISIS

Gas is a nice term for farts. Gas in a dog's stomach usually comes out as a fart, and farts become a big part of sharing one's life with our dogs. Farts precede poop and poop is especially interesting for a Dog Chef. Yogi and I will discuss more about farts and poop in the next exciting chapter called BECOMING A POOP DETECTIVE.

Bloat is a real canine crisis and needs to be continuously watched for in any dog, but especially dogs that are giant breeds and deep-chested. There are many breeds and their mixes that fit that picture such as Great Danes, German Shepherds, Saint Bernards, Labs, Irish Wolfhounds, Great Pyrenees, Boxers, Weimaraners, Old English Sheepdogs, Irish Setters, Bloodhounds, Standard Poodles, and Chinese Shar Peis. But don't be fooled that only these type dogs can get bloat, any dog can develop it.

What is bloat? It is a gastric problem that makes the stomach dilate and enlarge. Usually the combination of air, food, and water is present in the stomach when bloat occurs.

The dog might have a tendency to eat his food too quickly, thus swallowing a large amount of air. Some studies have suggested that it's best to hold off exercising your dog for at least thirty minutes after eating to keep him from getting bloat. Other dogs might benefit from eating from a raised bowl in a tall feeding table.

None of these precautions can absolutely prevent bloat, but if your dog has a tendency toward it, take note and use caution. Feeding your dog a natural diet is also not a sure prevention of bloat, but is a better solution than commercial dog food.

Bloat is one of those true emergencies which involves quick thinking on you and your veterinarian's part.

COOKING FOR TWO OR MORE

Multiple dog households can be handled easier if the dogs are eating more raw foods than cooked. Because each dog is likely to be at a different stage in its life, a Dog Chef could find themselves spending a lot of time in their kitchen if they are cooking their dog's food instead of serving it raw.

Buying frozen raw food from one of our resources in the Resource Guide can help a Dog Chef who has several dogs of different ages or states of health. Add that to a muesli or good quality dog food or cook up large batches of rice or barley, along with an addition of vegetables in season, and life can be easier and healthier for all of your dogs.

Supplements would be the only difference in each dog's food dish, other than the addition of raw bones. If one dog is older and doesn't have any teeth left to chew, than getting a food grinder to grind up the bones can be a real smart Dog Chef investment. After the bone is ground up, add it to your dogs meal and use that as the valuable mineral supplement any dog needs.

SPEAKING OF OLD FARTS - THE AGING DOG

Old farts come out of old dogs, or senior dogs might be a more polite term. Our senior dogs need special care, just like when they were babies. With more of an emphasis on quantity and quality when we are feeding a puppy, an aging dog needs more quality and less quantity. Even when you are feeding a senior dog a natural diet, their system will still become less efficient and their production of digestive enzymes slows down as they slow down.

Raw food is a much better bet for an older dog because less digestion has to take place. Also additional digestive enzymes added to your aging dog's diet can help him to extract more nutrients from the good diet you are feeding him which will nourish his body systems. There are many digestive enzymes or non-dairy probiotics, like Prozyme, that are made for animals, found in health food stores that can help your dog. See our Resource Guide.

Giving smaller meals and serving them two to three times a day is beneficial, along with some additional supplements to keep vitamins and minerals in the dogs' system throughout the day. And of course, we are **assuming** that you will be exercising your senior pal on a daily basis.

LOOKING THROUGH ROSE COLORED GLASSES

Master Dog Chefs view each dog in their life as an exciting opportunity to challenge their skills. They know that each individual dog, whether a pure bred or a mix, will have different nutritional needs. Those nutritional needs are affected by some of the following:

Where did your dog come from? His heritage, his breed? Every breed of dog, whether pure bred or not, has inherited different problems or needs regarding nutrition. Obtaining a guide book to dog breeds is a smart Dog Chef investment, since the good ones will list some of the inherited breed problems. Many of these guides include mixed breeds also. Learning the closest native environment of your dog can give you an idea of a diet that most resembles its native food.

Yogi is the sixth Chinese Shar Pei that has lived full time in our household. Shar Peis have inherited many problems, many of which come from poor breeding practices. Their most common problem is a fungal skin disorder, making their fur appear moth eaten and mangy. None of our Shar Peis have ever had that problem. Several have come to us in that condition, but it doesn't last. We attribute that to the feeding of a natural diet.

Shar Peis came from China and were brought to the United States in 1976. Not a long enough period of time for the breed to adjust to the heavy SADD (Standard American Dog Diet) in this country. In fact, William Cusick, author of CHOOSING THE BEST FOOD FOR YOUR BREED OF DOG, states, "The length of time needed to make a nutritional requirement change due to exposure to a new environment's food supply can take thousands of years."

Yogi and his relatives all came from the original fifteen Shar Peis smuggled out of China and brought to the United States in 1976. To expect this breed to thrive on overly cooked, processed food, which was foreign to their stomachs, has been a grave mistake. Many of these dogs are put down each year because of serious immune disorders resulting in skin problems and a host of diseases.

Chinese Shar Peis are primitive dogs and must be fed primitively. There is also an improvement in their behavior that parallels the improvement in their health.

Learning your dog's heritage is as important as knowing your own. Even if your dog is a mix breed, it can still offer you clues.

The climate where you and your dog live. You might have noticed that your dog is more active in cooler weather than when it's warm. So, the most obvious consideration as a Dog Chef is to up his calorie intake in the winter and reduce it in the summer. If he's a working dog all year long, you will have to amend that a bit.

How old is your dog? Your dog's age will dramatically effect his nutritional needs. Obviously, puppies will need food for growth and their need to chew. Active, middle-age dogs will need enough food to maintain their energy level. Seniors will need to eat foods that are easily digestible and nutritious.

Does your dog rollerblade? Is he active? Does he play and exercise each day?

Exercise stimulates digestion and gets the body's organs moving and strengthens blood vessels and muscles. It increases your dogs need for better nutrition.

Is your dog under stress? Sometimes it's hard to believe that our dogs can be under stress when we hear them snore or watch them sleep, but many dogs are, and that effects their nutritional needs. A move to a new home, coming from the animal shelter, continual environmental stimulation, a new family member such as a baby, a boy/girl friend, dog training - anything new to a dog is stressful. Slightly higher protein levels will help for some.

Are you breeding your dog and becoming a grandparent? Both the male and the female that are being bred have increased nutritional needs. Fresh food works toward preventing many health problems during the period of time before and after the puppies are born. Even spaying and neutering your dog will cause a change in their nutritional needs.

How well does your dog deal with change? Changing your dog's diet too quickly is stressful for some dogs. If you know that your dog can eat anything than this will probably not be such a problem. If your dog has been on the same food for years, the change to home prepared meals may be great tasting, but his body may need a longer transition.

Sometimes that transition can create some alarming symptoms in your dog's body. Some symptoms might be loose or mucousy stools, bad breath, dirty ears and smelly body odor, increased shedding, or flaking of old skin. Even acne or pimples. This detoxification is most frequently seen during the first and second month of the introduction of a new diet. As bad as it appears, it's a positive sign. Severe or continued symptoms beyond a two month period might need a consultation with your vet.

Riding out that transitional period with continued fresh food is what separates a Dog Chef from a short order cook.

One note that is appropriate here is water intake. Every client we have ever had made the comment, upon the initial stage of food change, that their dog decreased his intake of water dramatically. If you notice it, don't panic. It is very common because fresh, raw food has more water content in it compared to dry kibble or semi-moist processed canned food. Both require the dog to drink more water to aid with digestion.

Water should always be available for your dog, even if it appears he is drinking less often. Water will help his body in the food change and with detoxification.

A FEW STRAYS

Before we end this chapter and move on to the more exciting discussion on poop, here are a couple of stray ideas that Dog Chefs can stuff in their chef hat.

Liver Sausage. Liver sausage is not exactly a Master Dog Chef's ideal food, but it can be used effectively to give a reluctant dog a pill or to entice a sick or finicky dog to eat. Buy a small amount of liver sausage and throw it out after two weeks in the refrigerator.

Yogi and I have used liver sausage to get stray dogs to come out from their hiding places. It is also great to use it to distract a dog in training or for photographs (rub a small amount on your hands and continue to run your hands over the dogs' nose and mouth to get them to ignore the camera and to lick their lips). To get a finicky dog to eat or get interested in new food, place a dollop of liver sausage in a small hole in the center of the food.

The advantages of liver sausage are its strong, irresistible smell. Master Dog Chefs do not use it for feeding their dog, since its list of ingredients is not prime and it is quite fattening, but it is a great convenience food to jumpstart a new relationship with a dog. In our Recipe chapter, Yogi has a quick way for you to make your own liver pate. But commercial liver sausage has a smell and an attraction that is not easily duplicated.

STRAY, NEW OR FOSTER DOGS. The best way to introduce and welcome a new dog to your home is to simmer some chicken or turkey in a pot of water just before the dog is brought into the house. Simmering the meat will let it's odor fill the house. Don't give the new dog any food right away. Let him walk through your house savoring the smells and getting his digestive system ready for a small taste of what life will be like for him in your home.

After his nervousness subsides and the other pets are introduced, give the new dog a small taste of food. If your new dog is a stray or being fostered and you have no idea of his previous life and background, be prepared for the food change to effect him. Adding a 1/2 teaspoon of liquid acidophilus to his food on a daily basis will help with his transition.

There is nothing more rewarding than the experience of feeding a foster dog nourishing food and receiving the rewards of those endeavors when he plants a wet kiss on the face of his chef!

All dogs don't look alike, or bark alike, or even poop alike. Be prepared to start anew with each dog that comes into your chef life. Food is a wonderful way for us to "talk" with our dogs. We must understand that dietary changes and nutritional supplements are not total cure-alls for everything that ails our dogs, but if we learn how to use healthy food to speak with our pals, we may be surprised what they tell us!

CHAPTER SIX

BECOMING A POOP DETECTIVE

Time to change hats and add a dash of spice to your Dog Chef experience. This chapter is all about poop - dog poop! As a Dog Chef, looking at your dog's poop and observing him in the act, is one of the things that separates you from a people chef. Dog-poop-watching is truly the best way to see how the food we have chosen to feed our dog is working for him.

As we have discussed in the previous chapter, we can expect some possible digestive problems in our dog if we are transitioning him from one diet to another. Some dogs make the transition without any internal problems, others don't, with diarrhea being the most common sign of disturbance.

The general Dog Chef rule for a healthy dog experiencing diarrhea or constipation, is twenty-four to thirty-six hours before there is a call to a vet to discuss other possible problems. That time period is shortened if the dog is a very young puppy, because of how quickly dehydration can set in.

MOVING RIGHT ALONG

A common place for health problems in our dog is his digestive system. The main players are your dog's esophagus, his stomach, and the small and large intestines. If it's typical that your dog suffers from diarrhea, constipation or farts, a digestive problem is probably the culprit.

Of course, we have to **assume** that if these problems have been ongoing for a while, that you have taken your dog to a vet to have the possibility of something more immediate and severe checked out.

The possibilities of diabetes, liver disease, intestinal parasites, or intestinal blockages due to swallowing foreign objects, like rawhide chews, toys, etc., can have adverse effects on your dog's digestion. But we are **assuming** once again, that you have already ruled this out with your vet and we can talk Dog Chef to Dog Chef.

Yogi and I believe that the largest percentage of digestive problems are from poor, processed food continuously given over long periods of time. But don't take our word for it, if your dog typically has problems with diarrhea and/or constipation which come and go as often as the garbage man, and he has been checked out by your vet, then food is his problem. Change his food and watch what happens.

MOM, WHERE DOES POOP COME FROM?

Waiting in line at a supermarket, I was entertained by a mother trying to explain to her three year old son where poop came from. It wasn't an easy experience for her because she was doing her best to keep the subject "clean" and avoid using words that the rest of us, within hearing distance, might cringe at, especially while buying food. She told the boy not to use the word "poop" but instead to say "feces".

An older man, standing in front of the mother, could not contain his frustration any longer at her inability to answer her son's continual flow of poop questions.

He looked straight at the young boy sitting in the grocery cart and said abruptly, "Poop comes from the Feces-Fairy in the Land of Body

Wastes. The more you eat, the more of it comes out, either with a bang, or a smoosh. And sometimes, it just doesn't want to come out and you gotta call in the carrot soldiers to move it through the hole."

The young boy's mother smiled an embarrassed smile and showed a sign of relief when it was the man's turn to check out his groceries. Before he left the cashier, the man added one more thought in the mind of the curious kid, "Now ask your mom where farts come from!"

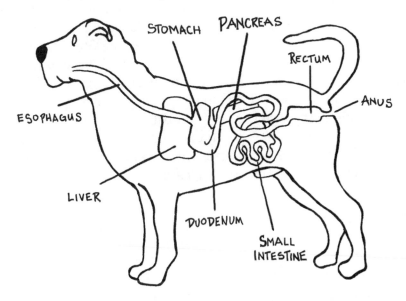

For those of you with the curiosity of a three year old boy, we'll dive into the subject of where your dog's poop comes from. We'll keep it light and non-technical and will leave words like "excrement," "feces," "stools," and "flatulence," to your vet. We will just use "poop" and "farts" to describe your dog's daily removal of wastes.

Your dog's poop comes from his body wastes. These are normal wastes that are useless to his body, including undigested food stuff. Healthy, flesh-eating animals, like your dog, poop out what they eat somewhere between four and eight hours. Humans, take much longer because of the 30 foot length of intestine that food has to pass through for digestion.

Your dog's large bowel finishes the job of the small intestines, absorbing water and nutrients from his food and wastes. Here's where poop is born and formed and where it is destined to come out as normal poop, as runny poop, or may even refuse to come out!

This is the area that is the first to give in to an overload of toxins. If your dog ate a lot of highly processed foods, they were not only lacking in nutrients but were also absent of fiber. Some fiber is good because it acts like a broom and sweeps the bowel clean of all of the junk, like accumulated mucus and waste buildup.

Some dog food diets have an excessive amount of fiber which is also associated with trouble "down-under." The result - loose, watery poop and farts. Insoluble carbohydrates (fiber that cannot be dissolved) tend to pass right through the dog because fiber absorbs water on its way through his scenic digestive tract and his body moves it out quickly. Heavier insoluble carbohydrate diets are commonly given to the bored or food-obsessed dog to give a feeling of fullness.

There are many other ways to tend to these problems with real food that makes the dog chew and is more nutrient based than overloading your dog's digestive system with too much fiber. His body can only compensate for the excess by creating loose poop.

WHAT ABOUT FARTS?

Before we continue this discussion on dog poop, we first need to concentrate on why dogs fart.

We can began by looking at this from a chef's point of view. If you're a rather messy chef and never clean your oven, spilled food and grease-splatter build up in the oven chamber. Pretty soon your oven smells and fills your kitchen with smoke when it's turned on. It won't get any better until you clean the inside.

Farts are a lot like the smoke in the messy chef's oven. Some smoke may normally eek out of an oven from regular use. Just as the production of gas in your dog's digestive tract is normal. But when it is excessive, smelly gas, that is when we need to pay attention and clean out the "oven."

Living with a chronically farting dog can be challenging! Excessive farts can be the result of the type of food eaten or from a problem in his digestive system.

Omnivores, like our dogs, tend to have gases form in their digestive systems which rely on bacterial activity for digestion of the plant stuff that they eat. When we feed our dog many types of vegetables like beans, cabbage, broccoli, and onions, for example, the gas can get pretty smelly. For some dogs, these plant materials are not easily digestible and they pass through the system a lot slower than other food.

Increased fermentation occurs when there is too much growth of bacteria in the digestive tract due to problems of the stomach, pancreas or intestines, including worms. These problems do not allow the digestive system to work as designed and the food stays in the system much longer, building up the fermentation. The result - farts - rotten, putrid farts.

If your dog continually has smelly farts, then you need to look for the root cause, since excessive farting is a symptom. Low quality dog food that contains a lot of vegetable material or continuously feeding the same food each day are big fart producers. Experiment with different food to see which food is the culprit. It might be that certain vegetables are difficult for your dog's digestive system if you are feeding him home prepared meals and he's still farting.

Animal proteins, such as meat and fats are digested quite quickly by your dog, so they should not produce an excess of gas. However, if they do, the problem might not be the kind of food but rather a problem with the dog's digestive system.

Yogurt contains acidophilus, a "friendly" bacteria that is good to feed your dog a few times a week, or daily, if he is on antibiotics. Antibiotics lower the levels of the friendly bacteria that live in the intestines. Acidophilus helps keep the ratio of good and bad bacteria in check and can help with excess farts. When buying yogurt, always check the label and make sure you're buying one that has "live cultures" in it. There are lots of "phony" yogurts out there and if you don't buy the real thing you may be adding gas to your dog, not taking it away!

POOP DETECTING 101

After a few years of living with a dog, most of us become very familiar with our dog's pooping schedule and what he poops. There are some dogs that like to "poop alone," or are "shy-poopers." Or many people let their dog out the back door and don't bother to do a poop check on a weekly basis.

Fortunately, it's not the job of a people-chef to check their clients poop. But it is the task of a Dog Chef, especially a Master Dog Chef, to do it weekly, or more if the dog shows signs of discomfort.

DIARRHEA. Even Dog Chefs get diarrhea and even the Dog Chef's dog gets diarrhea. Diarrhea is one of those events that we find hard to forget, whether with ourselves or with our dogs.

Diarrhea is pretty "loosely" defined, but is generally considered to be poop with more water than usual. The poop is usually unformed, or just plain watery with a touch of brown color added for affect. But diarrhea can come in many other colors of the rainbow, like green and frothy, or pale and tan, or even dark or bright red, or black, tarlike, sticky poop.

Diarrhea can come gushing out of your dog like a newly tapped oil rig, or be as sudden as the click of a camera lens. You may have some warning with the sour smell of something gone seriously wrong in your dog's "oven."

At the time that your dog is having diarrhea, his body is responding to some irritation or disorder and his digestive system is in essence saying, "Get this stuff outta here - quick!"

Quickly pushing the irritant through with the contents of what's in the intestines at the time, is a wonderful defense mechanism Mother Nature gave us all - human or animal. What makes the poop so watery and unformed is the shear speed of passage through the large intestine, not giving the poop time to create a form other than loose and watery.

Here's where the detective part comes in. Most diarrhea in a healthy dog is from food, stress and nervousness or something foreign, like garbage. The color, smell and texture plays a big part in what you need to keep an eye out for. Small amounts of bright-red blood in the diarrhea is usually not as much of a concern as it appears.

Although very alarming, it is often caused by food that had inflamed the large bowel. Even something like stress can be a cause of the inflammation.

The kind of diarrhea that is black, tarlike, and sticky is not a good sign because it could mean bleeding in the small intestine. The tarlike substance in the poop is digested blood, which needs immediate care from your veterinarian. This suggests a serious problem like liver disease, ulcers, rat poisoning, or bone splinters that tear up the intestines.

Besides surveying the color and texture, diarrhea associated with persistent vomiting, lethargy, fever, loss of appetite, or a reluctance to drink are clues to make an appointment with your vet.

If your dog just has plain old-fashioned diarrhea, then resting his bowels for twenty four hours is the best bet. Then you can start him back to food very slowly and watch what happens. Honey and lemon juice with diced up garlic is great for a sour stomach. A bit of mashed up apple, discarding the skin, or cottage cheese and a small bit of boiled chicken with rice, ease the digestive system back to the real world.

The first time Yogi had his picture taken was his first diarrhea experience in our presence. He looked very cool on the outside but inside he was falling apart from the stress. He was not familiar with a camera and its flash. He had no choice but to run to a corner and gush out everything. A few hours later he was fine since he was far away from the culprit - that nasty camera.

Most of the time diarrhea is like a strange relative that you know will be back one day but you don't know why!

CONSTIPATION. "One dog's meat is another's poison." A correct diet for your dog is the only preventative for constipation AND the only way to remove the toxins that have accumulated in the bowels that are the usual cause for constipation. Those toxins we discussed earlier with diarrhea, that are rapidly pushed out of the dog's digestive system, do the opposite with constipation. They like the setup they created in the bowels and refuse to leave, no matter how much your dog strains to expel them. In fact, those toxins from the dog's waste matter repeatedly get reabsorbed into his bloodstream until the impacted poop gets pushed out of the bowel and finally leaves his body. It's easy to see why your dog might be a bit grumpy when he's constipated or he's not quite up to playing ball. His bloodstream is like a sewer, reabsorbing his waste matter and making him feel pretty lousy.

Some of the same factors that lead to constipation in people do the same with your dog. Things like stress, poor diet, lack of exercise lead to blocked or sluggish bowels. With highly processed dog food, the muscles of your dog's large bowel have nothing to push against to make the poop move out.

Of course, if you're poop-detecting with a dog that has constipation, you won't be finding much poop. It's still inside of him! If he's obviously straining, or what poop does come out is thin and flattened or there are long periods between pooping, then get back in the kitchen and change a few things.

Chalky poop that is dry is also a sign of constipation and a need to change your dog's food.

Increasing the fiber intake with foods like whole grains, vegetables, fruits and seeds are good. Increase exercise and try raw meat. Or sprinkle a 1/2 - 1 teaspoon of bran on his food once a day. You also might try adding some olive oil, a teaspoon to a tablespoon daily, depending on the size of the dog. Olive oil is safe and tonifies the colon while stimulating intestinal muscle contractions and it adds a lubricant to the impacted poop mass in your constipated dog's body. A tablespoon of powdered barley or wheat grass daily in his food is real good for relieving constipation and preventing it. Fruits, like prunes and berries, are great Dog Chef additions a couple of times a week.

Normal constipation is a warning light for the Dog Chef to pay attention and see what's not happening with your dog's digestive system. It's telling us that not everything that goes in, will always come out!

POOP DETECTING 202

Besides the obvious pooping problems such as diarrhea or constipation, our dog can tell us more on whether the food we have chosen to feed him is working or not working.

We suggest to clients that they can benefit a lot from looking at other dogs' poop if they are out for a hike somewhere. You don't need to sniff it like your dog does, but while he's sniffing, you can look. This will sharpen your Dog Chef eye for future encounters with your own dog's waste. If you live with one dog and he usually poops the same, than your poop detection skills will never be crafted.

We have taken clients on poop hikes in areas where we know we can find lots of dog poop. Dog parks are wonderful places to bone up on your poop detection skills.

In our search for poop, we commonly see the **runny and gelatinous** poop, which if analyzed, might detect an infestation of worms. The internal environment of that particular dog is similar to a restaurant that received a "D" in cleanliness from the Health Department.

Shut it down and start all over!

The most common poop we see, from coast to coast, is the **voluminous** poop. The kind that looks like it came from an elephant! Most of the time the poop is well formed and a chocolate-color brown. There's just a lot of it.

Voluminous poop can tell us that the dog has a big appetite, but also that he may be enzyme deficient or can't sufficiently digest the type of food that he's eating. His diet is more than likely heavy in fiber and short on the nutritional end of the scale. This type of poop is most common because it reveals the typical commercial dog food diet that is generally fed to most dogs.

The problem with seeing this type of dog poop is that this diet will work for the dog for the younger years of his life. When he gets older and slows down, so will his digestive system and the start of many common digestive problems will begin.

Digestibility in the commercial dog food market is a never-ending, controversial subject that will go on as long as there is commercial dog food. You can take a whiff of the controversy by reading many different commercial dog food labels and bags. You won't have to look far before the word "complete" shows up in the ad copy on the bag.

The digestibility war can look very silly if you consider what these companies are striving for: "100% completeness." So if a commercial dog food is "proven" to be 100% complete in the area of digestibility, does that mean that the dog will not have any poop output? In other words, buy this food and feed it to your dog and he will never poop again! That would be the greatest discovery of the 21st century!

But is that what we want and would that be healthy? Of course we know that nothing in this world can ever be 100% complete, especially a science like nutrition. Whatever studies that were done for digestibility for any dog food were controlled studies that don't work in real life. Ignore any and all claims of complete and balanced anything. If you choose to believe those claims, then Yogi and I have a nice big bridge to sell to you in San Francisco!

EATING POOP AND LOVING IT!

A very common poop problem is the dog that eats poop. Not only his, but most other dog poop. These kind of poop-eaters even cross the canine line and eat cat poop - and love it! Or so it seems!

Poop eating has a fancy name like **coprophagia**, which you do not need to memorize. If your dog has this problem than just describing him as a "poop-eater" is sufficient and many people will be empathetic.

Poop eating is one of those subjects that is talked about in hushed tones but is as common as fleas. What would Aunt Martha think of your beloved little Pixie, who she lets smother her face in wet kisses, if she knew what little Pixie did in her free time?

Speaking of "free time," sometimes a poop eater eats poop because he's bored and has a lot of free time to roam the neighborhood and pick up a few souvenirs along the way. If your dog is a known poop-eater then giving him more attention or training, may change some of his ways. And most definitely he should not be roaming the neighborhood, no matter what his problem is.

Yogi and I have yet to see the dog that doesn't stop eating poop when fed a nutritional home prepared diet. When a dog is nutritionally "starving" they follow their instincts and find what they need. Cat poop is a special delicacy because of the large amount of protein in a normal cats diet.

You can put five experts on dog behavior in one room and discuss poop eating and come out with five opinions on the subject. From a Master Dog Chef's point of view, if your dog eats poop, than feed him a better diet and you'll notice he'll leave the poop on the ground.

PICK IT UP!

Before we end this chapter on poop detecting, there is one more thing you must do with your dog's poop - **pick it up!**

We just discussed why it's not a good idea for your dog to pick up poop because he generally will eat it. So the bag gets passed to you!

A Master Dog Chef wants everyone to enjoy and appreciate their dog like they do. Sometimes that's hard if your neighbor is left with

the part of your dog that no one could love, deposited on their lawn. It's not fair to your neighbor and it's not fair to your dog! Until that "100%-completely-digestible-zero-poop-output-commercial-dog-food" comes out on the market, your dog is going to poop and you need to **pick it up!**

CHAPTER SEVEN

DOGS AND THEIR CHEFS

What a pleasure it is to meet people who share and nourish their lives with dogs!

Have you ever noticed when you're at a dinner party, seated next to someone who you could never imagine you have anything in common with, when the magic words "my dog" comes out of their mouth and you look at them differently? Pretty soon, dog photos come out of wallets and purses and the stories began to flow like champagne.

Dog people are linked in many ways through dog training, agility, healing, walking, breeding and breeds, and we add - through food. The next few pages will introduce people and their dogs who are linked to this book through food. They are self-described Dog Chefs who have attained their Master Dog Chef status and their Common Sense Degree through their commitment and their desire **to nourish their dogs and themselves!** This again, is what separates a Master Dog Chef from a short order cook.

By the time a person reaches Master Dog Chef status, the realization that they are not only nourishing their dog with home prepared meals but they are nourishing themselves, becomes apparent, otherwise, they would not be doing it.

As you read about the following Master Dog Chefs, you'll find each one of them understanding the definition of nourishment by applying it throughout the various stages of their Dog Chef experience. Each of these people understood at some point that feeding their dogs good food was important, but so was taking charge of their dog's well being. These are people who question what their vet may suggest, either publicly or privately.

TO NOURISH: 1. to feed and cause to grow, to supply with matter necessary to life and growth. 2. to support. 3. to supply the means of support and increase to; to encourage; as, to nourish rebellion. 4. to cherish, to comfort. 5. to educate; to instruct. And to use common sense.

They know their dog best and they don't get caught up in believing what commercial dog food companies try to sell or tell them from their orchestrated studies. These people have done their own "studies."

Our Master Dog Chefs lead busy, productive lives and manage to fit their dog's nourishment in on a daily basis. They are all independent in choice, open minded in thought, and enthusiastic in life, and best of all, humored by their feeding experiments. They also share an important ingredient of the understanding of nourishment - common sense! When it comes to their dogs, these Dog Chefs are masters in common sense. They watch, listen, experiment, and they change!

Each Master Dog Chef interviewed had their own unique way of feeding their dog(s). Each one was well versed on the subject of home prepared meals, having read the "classics" on natural care and feeding of a dog. From there, they created their own form of meals. They know that there is no "one" recipe or way of feeding every dog and they respect that in each other.

To know a Master Dog Chef is to love them. You can bet that their house always smells inviting and there is a spark of mischief in their eye - kinda like a dog!

THE WAGNER HOUSEHOLD

The moment I walked into the kitchen of the Wagner's house, I desperately wanted to be one of their dogs. It was warm and cozy, well-lit but soft on the eyes, especially eyes peeking up from Cocker Spaniel level. It also smelled wonderful!

I was elated that the nice Wagner folks were making special muffins or a morning loaf just for my enjoyment while I interviewed them.

As Gary pulled the golden brown loaf out of the oven, I salivated like one of my Shar Peis. Drooled was more like it, but I caught the slippery-stuff with my tongue before it ran down my chin like my dog, Yogi.

When Gary walked past me without an offering, I was still convinced that this perfect loaf would be satisfying my hunger pains as soon as it cooled. It was fine with me when he broke off an end piece to share with one of the anxious Cockers. There was plenty for all of us.

I must confess that I thought Gary had taken this too far after he cut the loaf up into seven parts and wrapped it in plastic bags marked

"Peaches". Peaches is the youngest of his two Cocker Spaniels. This loaf is the mainstay of her daily food and, at the moment, the nice Mr. Wagner was not interested in being hospitable to me.

At the Wagner house, home cooking for their dogs is serious business. "Move over," "get out of the way," "don't touch that," were commands yelled out to me, not the dogs. The dogs knew the drill, I didn't. Gary barked out ingredients to no one in particular while he kneaded the next loaf for the older dog, Saucy.

Gary and Julie Wagner have a history of being Dog Chefs, dating back to a time when they lived in Italy. They shared their meals with two other Cocker Spaniels. At the time, Julie assumed the role of Master Dog Chef. Each day she shopped at the market for her, and Gary, and the two dogs. Commercial dog food was nonexistent in Italy.

Back in the United States, the Wagners vacillated back and forth from home cooking for their dogs to giving them what they considered to be the best commercial dog food. When Saucy, age fourteen, started to deteriorate from old age and a cancerous tumor was discovered between her eyes, the Wagners became "born again" home cooking addicts.

Gary surfed the Internet for a canine nutritionist and found one. For $25 per dog and several exchanges of email information of each dog's veterinarian history charts, an individual food program was set up.

Every weekend the ritual is repeated, a seven day supply is cooked, bagged and refrigerated, but not frozen. The cooking endeavor takes about three to four hours weekly, not including the shopping end of it. Gary is a good schmoozer with his local butcher. His chicken meat is deboned, wrapped in the familiar white butcher paper marked with his name and waiting faithfully for him weekly on Fridays.

"If you're not into this," Gary says, "it could really be a pain in the you-know-what, but I love it !"

PEACHES

ALL IN THE FAMILY

Pushing the door open, six dogs welcomed me as I walked into the bungalow, though not a human was to be found. The dogs sniffed me from ankle to crotch, than ran toward the rear of the older house into the big kitchen. The three ladies I had come to meet sat talking at the kitchen table, oblivious to the flurry of paws announcing my arrival.

My humanness finally stood out amongst the canine majority. I imagined what Thanksgiving was like in this close family of two sisters, a sister-in-law, their six dogs, husbands and half dozen children.

To an outsider, it was chaos - friendly chaos. After the dogs and I settled down, the munchies were passed around and introductions out of the way, the sharing began.

I felt a part of a big family where communication is done the old fashioned way, you jump in at any opportunity!

Mary Ayers, a dog trainer by profession, had been the first in the family to home cook for her dogs. That was thirteen years ago. Since then sister, Cathie Loomis and sister-in-law, Susan Loomis followed.

It was only recently that the three ladies and their six dogs came "out of the closet" and told the world about their past. "We seldom told anyone, even our vets, about our home cooking practices," Mary said, "It was just a lot easier to shake our heads up and down when it came to talking about dog food and go about our business as usual."

Mary, Cathie, and Susan created their own support system amongst themselves. They get together frequently as a family and home prepared meals for their dogs is always on their top ten list to talk about. They share ideas, recipes, experiments, and more importantly, the desire to continue to do what they have been doing for a long time. The results are always in front of them begging for more.

Rocky, a ten year old Rottweiler/Lab, was fed home prepared meals by Cathie starting when he was five. Laika, age five, and her daughter Zala, age two, are Vizsla's that have been reared on home prepared meals by Susan. Mary's three dogs, Reina, seven years old, and Rosa seven years, both Australian cattle dogs and their sidekick Teasel, eight years, a spirited Jack Russell, were also all raised on home prepared meals. Each dog looked as healthy as the next one. It was quite an impressive pack!

The three ladies use Dr. Richard Pitcairns' book NATURAL

HEALTH FOR DOGS AND CATS, as their main reference. They also refer to Ian Billinghurst's book GIVE YOUR DOG A BONE for ideas on adding raw bones.

One gets the impression that Mary, Cathie, and Susan are three women who could never be independently swayed from their beliefs in home prepared meals for their six lucky dogs. But, one would easily see that their strength comes in numbers and their bond is as much from the nourishment they get, than the fact that they are related!

BORDER COLLIE CUISINE

Gloria Vence has always appreciated the way English writers, when writing about home cooking for dogs, refer to dog food as "dog fuel." She has been fueling her two Border Collies (Luke, twelve years old and Tasha, ten years) with home prepared meals for eleven years. Whatever the fuel, it is working!

Having never lived with dogs like Border Collies, who watch your every move, I was impressed with their energy and agility at their ages.

Luke was a year old when he had an epileptic seizure and his vet recommended heavy medication and canned food. Gloria disagreed with the vet and banned commercial dog food from her house and started "fueling" Luke instead.

This was nothing new in Gloria's life. Growing up in a small town in Croatia, she was the daughter of a veterinarian. Dog fuel there consisted of raw bones, raw meat, pasta with red sauce, and potatoes and root vegetables. She went to school in Italy, where dog fuel was also very common.

Gloria is as intense as her Border Collies when it comes to reading anything on the subject of home prepared meals for dogs. Her library has every book ever written on the subject and she is like a walking encyclopedia on what works and what doesn't work when it comes to feeding her dogs.

Luke and Tasha eat a large variety of food each week, including short ribs with carrots, beets with potatoes in milk, and cabbage, alternating with rice and pasta. Gloria usually cooks every three days. She also gives both dogs raw bones and keeps the meat on the raw side.

When she brought Tasha home for the first time, she contacted a

human nutritionist at the University of California at Davis, for advice on raising Tasha as a puppy. Gloria has drawn on a lifelong experience of raising her two beautiful, healthy dogs without the claims of commercial dog food. It obviously all comes down to a better grade of fuel!

FREDD'S GOOD KARMA

When I first met Fredd, he wasn't laughing. Neither was his owner, Don Ray. Fredd was as cute as a Terrier mix could get, with wiry fur that knew no boundaries. You just want to squeeze him since he reminds many of us of the "dog next door."

Fredd would have no part in hugs from most humans or animals, except the ones he already knew. He liked Don and his wife Debra, their pet cat, and a few of Don's artist friends who wandered in his studio, but not without being greeted by a growl from Fredd.

Don talked to me about Fredd one day.

"He's an old sourpuss, he growls a lot and has been chewing himself to death."

We both looked at Fredd who didn't seem to care what names Don called him because he was mad and miserable.

Don and I plotted out a food plan for Fredd that would make him think he died and went to heaven. Fredd was in for one major change in his life and if food didn't make him change, then because of Fredd's behavior with people who came into the studio, he was going to have to stay home and sit in the yard.

Fredd had been in and out of the vet for his scratching and chewing and even discussions on his snappy behavior. But Fredd was not happy and nothing worked.

A few days after Don started giving Fredd home prepared meals, he called me and was cautious yet excited that Fredd had an overnight personality change. Best of all, Fredd was no longer scratching or chewing himself like he used to. A few more changes in Fredd's diet made this one grouchy Terrier a pleasure to be around.

Fredd continued to watch the door of Don's studio but he wagged his tail when someone entered instead of barring his teeth. Even as a Terrier mix, Fredd's sensitive system needed more raw and less processed food. His body appreciated the extra nutrients and was

relieved of his excessive scratching.

Through better nutrition, Fredd has gotten in touch once again, with his inner puppy and much better karma!

BULLIE HEAVEN

I knew I entered Bullie Heaven by the sticky nose prints on the window near the front door. It was there, peering through a slit in the drawn curtain, where one of the oddest dog faces on this planet greeted me. Five Bull Terriers and their chef, Jan Dykema, were in the middle of home prepared meals when I arrived. It was obvious by the wonderful smells coming from the kitchen, but most obvious from the dog's noses, smeared with food.

I felt right at home because living with Chinese Shar Peis is quite similar, feeding time gets messy. Another limelight Bull Terriers share with the Chinese Shar Pei are the host of physical problems built into their immune systems at birth. But the "Bullies" at Jan Dykemas' household live in Heaven, or so it must seem to them.

Jan has been home preparing meals for her Bull Terriers, ranging from puppies to ten years old, for many years. She breeds and shows her Bull Terriers, ever watchful of their changing bodies and nutritional needs.

When you show up at the Bullie House, whatever you ate three hours earlier will be sniffed out of you by their bulbous noses. Jan's Bull Terriers love their food and because of the myriad health problems they could get, she diligently follows Dr. Pitcairns' food plan from his book NATURAL HEALTH FOR DOGS AND CATS and combines his program with one that fits for the Bull Terrier breed. She also uses homeopathic medicines.

Jan's kitchen is cluttered with large pots often filled with food being cooked or prepared. The Bullies love the kitchen and spend much of their time surrounding Jan while she cooks. It's a never ending job creating home prepared meals for Sharkie, Sable, Roadie, Sam, and Jazz, but Jan loves it! And it's obvious.

The effort that goes into the healthy breeding and showing of these friendly dogs is daunting. When you catch one of them staring at you with their small eyes, you know they're communicating one thing - welcome to Heaven!

JAN AND TWO "BULLIES"

THE
DANES

COOKING FOR GIANTS

Patti Mattera is not a big woman, but she cooks for giants. They have big bowls, big toys, and big hearts. Patti's four Great Dane's; Spirit, Morning Glory, Sunshine, and Kismet, can scare the life out of you until you experience how they'll lick you anywhere they can find skin!

When I first arrived, Patti told me that the dogs were very friendly, but she would be letting them out in pairs. It became obvious why she chose to do it that way. These dogs love people and compete for your attention. It was a good way to see each dog up close and personal, since their eye level was almost at the same as my own. I got to pet their sleek, black, seal-like coats and admire their uncropped ears.

After I was introduced to all four Danes, Patti rattled the dog cookie jar, where their interest in me was replaced by homemade cookies. She showed me her kitchen, which was setup very efficiently for cooking in large batches for her dogs. Her big refrigerator housed different kinds of meats and labeled containers of leftovers.

Patti is very methodical in her approach to home prepared dog meals. She has read most of the books on home cooking and follows several different plans to fit her giant dogs. She experiments a lot and has learned in her many years of home cooking to be versatile and not stick to just one diet.

Patti learned her lesson through traveling with her dogs to dog shows. Getting stuck a few times in the middle of no where without available food for the Danes made Patti more adaptable than most Dog Chefs.

She has learned to incorporate commercial dog food into her dogs' diets before they leave on a trip, just in case the inevitable happens. Patti and her husband, Nick, have shown and bred their beautiful Great Danes for many years. The pictures on the walls reveal the lineage that goes way back in time. Each one of Patti's puppies were raised on home prepared meals and have lived a long and healthy life.

For over a dozen years, Patti has been fostering Great Danes through a rescue program. Her passion for the breed and her responsible breeding practices fit into the nourishing atmosphere of her house of giants!

THE NOBLE SCOTTS

Eva and Andrew LaMar - Friedlund enjoy the company of two fine Scottish Deerhounds, Qwilleran and Rebel. There is something paradoxical about Scottish Deerhounds. It's their quiet and dignified character along with their slow movements. But if left to chase an invader in the yard, they can move like the wind.

The beauty and grace of their gait is also confused by their wiry, shaggy fur and rather comical faces.

Eva and Andrew are the newest Master Dog Chefs amongst our group. But they have jumped in with both feet and have made home prepared meals a real family experience. They love sharing their meals and their mealtime with their two Deerhounds, especially on lazy Sunday mornings when they all enjoy eggs and whatever else is found in the kitchen.

The dogs are fed organic meat along with vegetables such as carrots, zucchini, or squash. They have oatmeal or wheat waffles for breakfast with chicken necks and backs. And they get raw bones to brush their teeth.

Eva also uses Flint River dog food kibble four times a week mixed in with raw organ meat or ground meat, eggs and fresh fruit for dinner. Eva and Andrew have read the Pitcairn and Billinghurst books and follow their advice closely.

Eva orders raw, organic frozen meat delivered to her house from Grandad's of Santa Clara, California (see Resources).

The beauty and dignity of these two wonderful dogs is affectionately brought out by their two devoted humans.

CHAPTER EIGHT

VACATIONS, CAMPING TRIPS, EARTHQUAKES ... OH, MY!

Can you still be a Dog Chef for your dog while taking him on vacation? You betcha! How about a camping trip? That's a natural. What happens during an earthquake or a hurricane? If you're prepared and your house isn't wiped off this planet, your dog will think he's on vacation.

If you're going on a vacation or camping trip with your dog or you're preparing for natural disasters, planning ahead is the key. The good thing about storing food and water for your dog in a possible natural disaster is that you can use that food and water to take with you on a vacation or camping trip. It's important to change the stored food and water every two - three months anyway. That's also a good excuse to take a vacation every few months!

Replace the stored food and water with more food and water. It's not more expensive, since you would have to buy food before you leave on your trip anyway. It also is very wise to be prepared for the unknown for yourself and your dog, especially if you live in an area where natural disasters commonly occur or are predicted to occur, like California.

EARTHQUAKES AND THOSE NASTY HURRICANES

Most anyone who has lived in California for at least ten years is familiar with the sensation of the earth moving beneath their feet or their house shaking for a few seconds. Almost every day in California there is an earthquake somewhere in the State, most of which are not felt or are located in less populated areas.

In 1989, the San Francisco Bay Area was hit with a major earthquake that paralyzed many neighborhoods for a week or two and took several months to restore life as most everyone knew it. If a Dog Chef had prepared for that earthquake it would have depended on how badly damaged their house was to know if the supplies they had stored would be usable.

There are no guarantees that your food and water will be there for you and your dog during a disaster, but you are a wise soul for making the effort. Consider using a storage area in your house or garage, utilizing a heavy duty camping cooler or durable rubber garbage cans for stocking your supplies.

Hurricanes offer the same unpredictability. Even if your house is not damaged in an earthquake or a hurricane, but the disaster has created havoc in your surrounding area, it can be days before the meat truck or the pet food van comes rolling back into your neighborhood.

A MENU FOR DISASTER

Whether the area where you live has experienced a tornado, an ice storm, or ten feet of snow, you can't count on your refrigerator since a power outage is realistic. If you have frozen meat in the freezer, let it thaw on it's own and use it in raw form for your dog. If you have more meat than you can use in one day, than obviously it will go bad and need to be thrown out after a day of thawing and no refrigeration. If you do have a way to cook over a woodstove or fire than cooking the meat will give you one extra day of use.

We keep three durable rubber garbage cans with lids in a secure storage area with food and water for pets and people. There are water jugs in each garbage can, which are rotated with new ones every two months. We mark ahead on our calendar when we need to change our water, which makes it easier to remember.

Canned commercial dog food and dry kibble are also stored in our cans but they have to be changed more often in areas where the humidity or dampness can affect them. Our favorite items are the freeze-dried pet products or the fermented meat products like BalanceDiet. You can find all of these products listed in the Resources.

Adding a two week supply of natural food vitamin supplements is a good idea. Buy the kind that are in a chewable tablet form. We use Fresh Factors for dogs and store a couple dozen in a zip lock bag, trading them on occasion with a new batch. These supplements can help your dog during this stressful period.

Another item to keep adding to your freezer every so often are raw bones. Bag them in a zip lock freezer bag and if there is a disaster and the power goes out, letting your dog chew bones can help with his hunger and his frustration.

VACATIONING WITH FREDD

Taking your dog with you, to just about anywhere in the United States today, is a breeze. Hotels and motels, and even some B & B's, offer wonderful accommodations for you and your dog. Or you might travel in an RV which is very accommodating since RV parks expect many people to have dogs. It's great fun to meet the traveling public in an RV.

Once we met an older couple traveling with their two parrots and a Brittany Spaniel. It was fun to see how they had created a special space for the three pets in their RV. The dog had a kennel built into a cabinet where she slept and where they contained her while driving in risky conditions. Otherwise she was free to roam the large motorhome. The parrots also had built in cages and areas outside of their cage where they could get a change of scenery.

The woman, Carol, was a Master Dog Chef for sure. She had made RV-prepared meals for many years. She couldn't recall how long it had been since she had opened a bag of dog food, or even commercial parrot food. She fed her pets what was available in the area where they were staying.

Carol said that when they first started on the road, she tried hard to stick to a special diet for the three pets, but it became impossible.

"I had a few terrifying experiences where everything went bad in the

humidity of Florida and in North Dakota, all of our supplies froze up."

Carol surrendered to the RV gods and went with the flow of the road. She pursued Farmers' Markets wherever she could find them and taught herself to schmooze with butchers from the mountains to the sea. In between, she had the foresight to prepare dried food she made from her own food dehydrator.

Carol's dog Mindy is a spirited eleven year old with bright, clear eyes and a sleek coat. She is disease free and suffers no joint problems.

If you're an organized Dog Chef like Carol, RVing with your dog can be simple, thanks to propane refrigerators and electrical plug-ins at parks. But motel hopping and camping take a bit more creativity.

WE'LL LEAVE THE LIGHT ON

There are many books written on the subject of where to stay with your dog. No matter whether you're staying at Motel Six (who usually allows pets to stay) or a much swankier hotel, feeding your dog hotel-prepared meals can still happen. You will, of course, need to bring a small suitcase or backpack of your dog's supplies. Consider the following:
. water and food bowel
. fork and a good cutting knife
. small plastic cutting board
. Simple Green or white vinegar for cleaning
. vitamin/mineral supplemental wafers or chewable tablets
. handiwrap, a plastic container and zip-lock bags
. Rescue Remedy Flower Essence (for calming, trauma, new situ
  ations)
. 3 or 4 blue ice packs
. old bones or toys to chew
. the dog's blanket or bed
. a roll of paper towels
. 2 to 3 bottles of water, preferably from your home tap water

When traveling with your dog, it's best to carry water in bottles from your home or buy bottled water. Every city has it's own formula for cleaning their water supply. Sometimes that means a lot of chlorine or fluoride. If your dog drinks well water from your home and is not used to chlorine in his body, prepare for loose stools.

We either bring our own water or buy it along the way in bottled form. We also use a wonderful product called PET-LYTE from Nature's Path. PET-LYTE is a natural supplement that comes in a liquid electrolyte concentrate. It is recommended to help keep your pet hydrated while on the road (see our Resources).

The easiest way to give your dog meat is to buy it along the way. Unless you are intentionally going somewhere in the country where you know you will be far from a store, you will have no problem finding most major stores or small butcher shops close by. Ask the desk clerk or look in the yellow pages of the phone book for butcher shops or grocery stores. Some of the oddest places we have traveled to have caught us by surprise with wonderful old-fashioned butcher shops or stores with clean meat markets. We have also found organic farms listed in the phone book that sell meat or eggs. Before you leave for your trip, send for a National Farmers' Market Directory (see Resources). Take advantage of your tax paying dollars!

You can stop at the store before or after you check in to your room. Buy what you need for that day and the next if you have a refrigerator in your accommodations. If you do, put your blue ice packs in the freezer section to use for the next day's travel. That way you can save yourself a daily trip to the store. Pack your meat with the ice packs in a small cooler the next morning and take it along for an afternoon snack or a meal for your dog.

There are many healthy convenient foods to travel with as a replacement for your dog's fresh meat that do not require refrigeration, but should always be kept in an airtight container out of the direct sun and heat. Some good ones are:

. fermented meat like BalanceDiet
. freeze-Dried Meat like Steve's Real Food For Dogs
. a Pet food pre-mix or muesli like Sojourner Farms or Monzie's Organics or Noah's Kingdom (can be mixed with hot water for daily individual servings and fresh meat added).

These products can be shipped directly to your home before you leave. It is always best to integrate them into your dog's diet at least a week or two before you hit the road.

If you are carrying a cooler with you and can freeze the blue ice packs and refrigerate the food nightly, than you can use the following convenient products:
- compressed meat loaf like Red Barn
- Grandad's or FeedThis Frozen Meat
- raw meat knuckle bones

ROAD FOOD

Here are some other road food suggestions for you and your dog to share at rest stops.

How about trying:
- hard boiled eggs
- raw nuts and seeds (preferably unsalted and no peanuts. Peanuts are not true nuts, but are legumes and may contain a carcinogenic aflatoxin and cause an allergy. Pumpkin seeds are wonderful and can be dried yourself, they have many vitamins needed by your dog).
- fruit: Watermelon, grapes, apples, pears, bananas. Or dried unsulphured fruit. (You can dry your own at home with a food dehydrator. Feed in moderation and don't give to your dog if he already has loose stools! Dried fruit is high in natural sugar and moisture and is digested very quickly). Always feed fruit to your dog separate or at least a 1/2 hour away from other foods or it may speed them through the digestive system too quickly and cause stomach upset.
- veggies: Carrots, celery, tomatoes, jicama
- rice
- yogurt (always good for any road trip because of the different food and water your dog will be exposed to and great for diarrhea. The benign organisms in yogurt can destroy strains of E. coli. Look for the words "live cultures" on the container or label, they have the beneficial bacteria).
- raw honey on whole wheat bread
- Gator Aid (good for dogs that might feel sick driving through mountain roads or the desert heat. A good hydrator, put a small amount mixed in with their water or let them drink it on their

own. Don't overdo).

- Zuke's Power Bones (a formulated food energy bar for your dog - a wonderful snack food that can be purchased at health food stores or mail order).
- fruit juice bars (made from actual fruit such as peaches, strawberries, etc. found in the freezer section of health food stores. Great for taking a break from those long, dusty roads).
- unsalted, unbuttered popcorn. Buy a small air popper to carry with you and a jar of popcorn. Each morning you can pop popcorn for your travel that day. Add a tad of unsalted butter and a teaspoon of raw honey blended in with the popcorn to create popcorn balls. Your dog will have a great treat to eat and play with when you stop at a rest stop to enjoy your lunch).

If you are really, *really* desperate, you can stop at McDonalds or Wendy's and buy your dog a hamburger without the mayonnaise and sauce. If your dog has a raw-meat-stomach, this meal will not go over very well and should be skipped. Master Dog Chefs do not recommend too many stops at fast food establishments, *only if you are really desperate*, they are everywhere.

For some dogs, hummus, a Middle Eastern spread made from chick peas and olive oil, is very good and acceptable. It can be spread on carrot sticks, celery sticks or bread. Make it at home or buy it ready made at any health food store.

If your dog travels well, meaning he doesn't throw up at every turn, then it's a good idea to feed him smaller meals along your journey. If he does get sick it's best to wait to get to your overnight stop before feeding him.

Always carry a small spice can of powdered ginger in your car for dogs that do get sick on the road. Wet your finger and dip it into the spice can, getting a small amount of ginger on your finger. Stick your finger in your dog's mouth or rub it along his lips. Ginger goes way back in history as an anti-nausea remedy and was used for astronauts for their moments of motion sickness. Great for taking your dog on a boat ride also.

CAMPIN' OUT

Camping with your dog means his own backpack with a few simple items like two collapsible bowls - one for water, the other for food. Bottled water is best, since your dog is as susceptible as you are to contacting the parasite giardia from mountain streams and rivers.

Most of the food in the previous section can apply to camping with the understanding that heat and the other elements, insects, rats and mice, raccoons, and bears are an added problem.

If you are camping by foot with your dog, bring along an herb or wild plant identification book, just in case a bear or raccoon happens to eat all of your food. The forest is a treasure trove of wild food, if you know what you're looking for!

To take our dog along with us wherever we go and still be able to practice the art of Dog Chefing only means we have to "gear up" for the event. In today's world someone has probably already made the product that will make your life easier to travel with your pal. Healthy and fresh dog food is springing up everywhere. It is possible for our pets to escort us from one adventure to another. I can picture it now, the window of the motorhome rolled down and Yogi's wrinkles flapping in the breeze! What a sight for sore eyes!

ᴌEFTOVERS

Yogi and I became friends in our kitchen. The kitchen is hard to beat when it comes to starting a relationship with a new dog or an older one who has been around for awhile but you want to get to know better. This is where the soul of friendship has been centered for most of mankind's evolution.

Food dates back to the beginning of time and is one need every human and animal have in common. We all require food.

Aromas from the kitchen arouse all kinds of emotions and thoughts that remind us of happier days. They can do the same for your dog. When Yogi came to our house from the animal shelter, I had a batch of simmered meat on the stove and veggies gently cooking in a bit of olive oil. He walked through the strange new doorway lead by his nose.

The kitchen is where he met his new housemates and where his life began with us, welcomed by the aromas of food that have bonded millions of humans and animals before our existence.

The intention of this book was not to complicate your life anymore than it probably already is, or to make you feel guilty for not always being diligent about what you are feeding your dog. Quite the opposite, feeling stressed and guilty occupies too much mental real estate to properly use the definition of nourishment and apply that to your dog.

If that's your case, it would be best for you to skip to our Resource guide and order a small quantity from two or three of the fresh dog food manufacturers listed and get your dog started on better food. When less stressful times avail themselves, you can take on a bigger part of the meal preparations. Meanwhile, you should see some amazing results with your dog and his health, and will be anxious to make more of a change.

Becoming the chef your dog thinks you are is based on timing. Whenever a person seeks the company of a dog, it is with good intentions. Those good intentions sometimes fall as flat as a souffle if we open the oven door too fast. Easing into home prepared meals and watching your dog's health ever so closely, is better than the all-

American attitude of "jump in and do it."

If you're good at jumping in with both feet, then do it! If not, take the souffle approach and open the door slowly.

The best way to gradually ease into feeding your dog with fresh food is to start by finding and building a relationship with a good butcher. Ask lots of questions and learn from his vast knowledge.

The next step is to read other books on home cooking for your dog. When reading these books, understand that many of these authors are "purists" in the subject and may suggest that you <u>must</u> jump in with both feet and you are a bad person if you don't. Keep one thing in mind: most everyone who ever had a dog, fed at least one of their dogs commercial dog food at some point in their life. And each one of us screwed up somewhere with our dogs! Why? Because - you guessed it - we're only human!

I have a story to tell you about my first experience with commercial dog food. I actually helped to promote it!

I was the ripe old age of seven. In our local grocery store was a display of the first canned dog food I ever saw. It was a promotion for VET'S dog food. To attract new customers, they created a campaign to appeal to dog lovers. This was in the prehistoric year of 1955. VET'S

dog food company offered to give a blind person a "seeing-eye" dog if the consumer saved up 100 labels of their can food and sent the labels to the main headquarters.

I was hooked and began saving up my canned dog food labels, but it wasn't an easy sell for my mother. She was convinced that what we were feeding our dogs was already good enough, so why should she believe that a dog food company could provide better nutrition? All of my relatives and our friends that had dogs, felt the same way.

It's a bit ironic, but the effort I put into convincing everyone I talked with to buy this commercial canned food was as big as the effort I'm putting in now to convince people to return to preparing home meals for their dog! Silly me! It's deja-vu, or it's now a chance to correct a good idea that got out of hand.

By the way, I did convince most of our relatives and friends that had dogs to save labels for me. In a matter of six months, I had my 100 labels and proudly sent them into the VET'S dog food company. They in turn sent me a certificate with the name of the seeing-eye dog that was given to a blind person.

My mother continued to buy VET'S dog food for our dogs after the campaign had ended and I did my good deed. The company had tugged at our heartstrings and led a successful promotion that changed the lives of many people and their dogs.

Labels were pretty simple in those days and ingredients did not have to be listed. But I do remember what the VET'S dog food label said, since I had over 100 of them in my possession; VET'S DOG FOOD - REAL FOOD FOR REAL DOGS!

Interesting choice of words and not something that could honestly be put on too many commercial dog foods today.

My mother continued to supplement other food along with the VET'S dog food for awhile, but the 1950's were the decade of convenience and soon our dogs lived only on commercial food from that point on.

I don't lay awake at night feeling bad about my early experience of promoting a dog food company to my unsuspecting relatives. I do have to remember when I'm talking with a client or doing a cooking seminar that shaking a finger at people who "don't get it" is not appropriate. I too, trusted that commercial dog food was the end-all of my dog's healthy life.

It's all a matter of timing. For me, it was many years later when my own health declined that I could see parallels with my dogs health. It's like Robert Louis Stevenson once said, "Old or young, we're all on our last cruise."

With that in mind, you decided to take this "last cruise" with your dog by your side. Shouldn't it be fun, exciting and full of adventure?

FIGHT DULLNESS - BECOME A DOG CHEF

If you compare the life of a short order cook to that of a chef, you will see a tremendous difference. The same can be said about a Dog Chef versus someone who hurriedly opens a can of dog food or pours out a bowl of kibble for their dog and leaves. A Dog Chef's life is never dull!

A Dog Chef never stops learning. They are on a path of continuous renewal with themselves and the relationship they have with their dog. Anyone can act harried and overwhelmed with their life and say they don't have time, because it is the national disease. People get up everyday and go through the motions, never remembering that, "Old or young, we're on our last cruise." A Dog Chef needs and wants their lives to mean something, especially with their dog!

A Dog Chef is eternally interested (which makes them very interesting!). They maintain a sense of curiosity, even when others throw cold water on new ideas. They discover new ways and new things to keep them motivated and fresh. They care - what's on a label and what is done out of convenience versus nourishment. They take risks, by ignoring the naysayers and going past the limitations and boundaries set by people with small minds and dissatisfaction with their own lives.

Dog Chefs know failure. They're also familiar with starting over - many times. They don't mind that their dog has seen them at their worst as a chef. He's been there when they turned on the blender without putting on the cap, or when the pots boiled over. Or when he was barely able to navigate his way through the kitchen because it was filled with too much smoke. Dog Chefs love that intimacy with their dog and their dog loves it too.

Dog Chefs have their own style which is very important for any chef. They understand that their style is unique to them and no one else. They have big hearts and "chefing" for dogs expands their big heart even more.

Dog Chefs are as whimsical and intuitive as their dogs. They don't carry a grudge and like their dogs, they are eternal optimists!

DOG CHEFS AND THEIR VETS

At Dog Chefs of America™, we are continually asked the same question, "As a Dog Chef how do you deal with a veterinarian?"

Our reply is, "What's there to deal with?"

Your veterinarian is just that, your veterinarian. Just like your butcher is your butcher, your mechanic is your mechanic, your priest or minister is your priest or minister. Your veterinarian can be whatever you make him or her to be. But remember, you are living with your dog. Until your vet moves into your house and lives with your dog, he's only a consultant for your dog.

Most people who have problems with their veterinarian create their problems.

Veterinarians are human beings who generally have a large clientele, their own families, their own lives, and even their own dogs. They went to school for a long time and learned the scientific side of dogs and unless they continually study nutrition on an ongoing basis, they are not experts on the subject. Veterinarians have opinions, that's for sure. But so do you. When two opinions don't jive, you vote with your feet and move on to another one.

We live in a small town and are lucky to have several veterinarians close by. We have mainly gone to the same one for over eighteen years, but are friends with a few others. Each vet we know has a different opinion, a different style, and we know it. We appreciate each one for who they are and enjoy them as our friends. We don't expect them to change their style for us and when their opinions don't match ours, we find the one that does.

"If you want surgery, you go to a surgeon." The same is with a veterinarian. If you want to home prepare meals for your dog and your vet throws cold water on it, find a vet who will support you in your thinking. If you can't find one right away, talk with other people who are home cooking for their dog or read a book on the subject just like you're reading this one and you will be led to the place where every kind of vet is available.

Your vet is harmless. He took a vow to "first, do no harm." If his attitude seems a bit threatening or arrogant, play like your dog and get goofy. Yogi runs circles in the driveway when we act too serious, like when we need to clean his ears. Run circles in your vets office, get playful and shake your head up and down. He'll be happy to let you out of his office.

Many people have weird expectations of their vet. They want his or her stamp of approval or anointment for every thing they do with or for their dog. You have no one to blame but yourself, you have created the monster!

Dog Chefs don't need permission to give their dogs **real food.** If you believe that you are nourishing your dog, then the proof will be in the pudding!

NOURISH YOUR DOG, THEN TAKE IT TO THE STREETS!

We have formed **DOG CHEFS of AMERICA**™ to spread the word on nourishing your dog and your soul through home prepared meals. We also want to collectively get Dog Chefs together, to support their home cooking efforts and have a good time doing it.

DOG CHEFS of AMERICA™ also believes in helping others who have the job of caring for the thousands of dogs who no longer have anyone to nourish them or never did.

We give 10% of our profits to pet rescues and encourage others to do the same. Don't just send money to an organization without specifying where that money is to be spent. If you specify, you are directing your dollars where you want them to work (too bad the IRS didn't work that way!).

You can go to our **DOG CHEFS of AMERICA**™ **web site at: www.dogchefs.com**

We can link you to many rescue agencies where money is always needed for dogs who are not as lucky as your dog. Please nourish your dog, then take it to the streets!

WHAT'S NEXT?

In this century we will see some major changes in our food and our dog's food. Food processing will make the biggest change. "Pulsated Electrical Field Preservation Techniques" will blow our present archaic way of food processing out of the water.

Short bursts of electrical pulses will inactivate bacterial spores for a longer period of time. That will make foods retain higher levels of vitamins and nutrients, and help them taste better and retain better firmness. This will make frozen foods a thing of the past, since foods will not need to be frozen or even kept cold during transportation because of this process.

This will change our lives like our ancestors changed their lives at the turn of the last century. It will make us more mobile, more able to go for longer periods of time without our dependence on our refrigerator.

Yogi and I see each town having their own Dog Food Maker. You've heard of Wine Makers? Watch for Dog Food Makers to become the career of the future. We see Master Dog Chefs like ourselves opening up Bistros in every major city where people and their dogs can go and chat and eat together.

We see homes designed "with the dog in mind," schools for dogs that act as day care centers as well as learning institutions. Healing centers where dogs will play and rest with people who are sick and stressed. They will replace high priced psychiatrists and sit in a chair and listen, something they do for free anyway.

It's fun to think of the future with our dogs. To think of the crazy things we can do with them and the incredible places we will be going with them. How about to the moon, Alice? Or a cruise for people and their dogs? The "poop-deck" would certainly become a reality there.

If all of this sounds a bit outlandish to you how about becoming the chef your dog thinks you are? It's never too late. Remember, "it's fine being a late bloomer, just don't miss the flower show!"

Bone Appetit from Micki and Yogi!

CHAPTER TEN

STRAIGHT FROM THE DOG'S MOUTH - YOGI'S RECIPES

This is a sampling of recipes that Yogi likes best. These recipes can be used intermittently or set up in a menu to suit your dog - **if he likes them!** There are many ways to use recipes. If you see an ingredient that you know does not agree with your dog, take it out or substitute it with one that does. Recipes are wonderful strategies to help us with the feeding of our dog. Remember, they are not written in chicken blood, so therefore, they can be changed!

There are lots of cute doggie biscuit recipes to be found. We're not excited about most of them because of the ingredients they use, such as: sugar, brown sugar, various flours and baking powder and salt.

Sugar of any kind is totally unnecessary for your dog. Many dogs like sugar and are even addicted to it because of the processed food they were reared on. Even honey or molasses that will be cooked in a recipe is not a good idea. Once the honey or molasses is heated it will lose it's rawness and turn to sugar in your dog's digestive system. We only use raw, unheated honey or molasses on a recipe after the creation has been cooked and cooled.

The ingredient, baking soda, is a nutritionally empty ingredient that is put in recipes to make the biscuit look good to US. We guarantee you that your dog won't care if his homemade biscuits are flat!

Salt can be good for your dog if he's on a totally raw food diet. But if you are still feeding your dog commercial dog food or even supplementing him with it, he is getting salt a plenty.

You will notice that we use a muesli mix for our flour base in most of the recipes. You can create you own, or buy some from a health food store (check the ingredients for added sugar) or buy a pre-mix from Monzie's Organics or Sojourner Farms, as listed in the Resource Guide.

We use Monzie's because they are close by and they create a good product, already pre-mixed. You just need to grind the mix in a blender to create a flour. Any leftover <u>ground</u> muesli must be refrigerated to preserve it.

Monzie's ingredients are organic oats, organic barley flakes, organic rye flakes, organic bulghur, organic flaxseeds, organic sesame seeds, organic sunflower seeds, kelp, carob, vegetable broth, garlic and parsley. It makes recipes quite simple and very natural.

Some of Yogi's recipes are not exact. Each time we have made the biscuit recipes with the meat base, we have come up with a different consistency. That's because if we say "add one chicken thigh with bone," that chicken thigh is not always proportionately the same. Sometimes it has a larger bone, more fat, less fat, no fat - you will just have to "wing it!" But, that's part of becoming a Master Dog Chef, right?

Our first recipes will give you the basis of making some raw dishes that can be frozen for future use.

YOGI'S PATES'

CHICKEN or TURKEY

Take a cut up raw chicken fryer and put an individual piece of the fryer in a food processor or blender at a time. Make sure your food processor or blender can handle cutting up chicken or turkey bones. Add a 1/4 cup of water with each piece.

Once each piece is pureed, pour into a large bowl. With the last piece, a clove or two of garlic can be added and a teaspoon or two of olive oil, depending on the size or the need of your dog.

We stir the entire batch by hand until blended well. Put into single serving freezer containers, marking the date and the dog's name on the container, along with what the type of pate it is. Remove one of the containers from the freezer a day in advance and let thaw in the refrigerator. If the container mix is still slightly frozen the next day, put it in a small bowl of warm water for a half an hour to thaw completely. Serve immediately with muesli dry dog food or by itself. Do not let this mixture thaw outside of the refrigerator or sit for several hours on your counter.

Remember, **WE** are the biggest cause of food poisoning because of our short- order-cook-behavior!

LIVER OR BEEF HEARTS

Raw liver and beef hearts can be made in the same fashion as the Chicken Pate, but with less worry whether your food processor or blender can handle the job. Add a sufficient amount of water to create a jello-like texture to your pate. You can also add the garlic and olive oil if desired.

These pates are very good for traveling in an RV where they can remain frozen in the motorhome freezer. They are wonderful for sick or weak dogs who need extra nutrition. They are great for dogs transitioning from an animal shelter and need extra calories and nutrition, and they are terrific backups for when you didn't plan anything for your dog that day. Yogi eats one serving of pate a week or more often if we are on the road.

DANDY'S FOUR PAW SOUP

4 large red bell peppers
4 cups beef broth
2 tbsp. olive oil
3/4 cup cream
4 medium carrots, diced
1 tbsp. grated lemon peel
1 medium potato, diced

1. Roast peppers over open flame if you have a gas stove, until skin blisters.

Immediately place in a paper bag, then place that bag into a plastic bag. Let sit for 10 minutes, then peel skin and remove seeds.

2. While peppers are cooling, saute carrots, potatoes, and add stock. Cover pan and cook over medium heat for 15 minutes or until carrots and potatoes are very tender.

3. Place peppers and carrot mixture into blender. Blend until smooth. Add cream and lemon peel. Reheat until just boiling. Remove from heat and into a large bowl. Add a small amount of chopped parsley on soup for better digestion, don't overdo. Serves 4 medium dogs (or 8 Chihuahuas!).

DO NOT SERVE HOT OR WARM - SERVE ROOM TEMPERATURE!

(Revised from a people recipe from the Livingston Foundation Cookbook by Ana Maria Canales).

CHICKEN RUN STOCK

2 pounds chicken backs
and necks
2 carrots, chopped
12 cups filtered water
2 celery stalks with
leaves, chopped

Combine all ingredients in a stock-pot. Bring to a boil over medium-high heat, reduce heat, partially cover, and simmer for 45 minutes. Strain the stock and discard solids. Refrigerate until ready to use. Makes 12 cups

(A Chicken Run or Turkey Run stock can be made using a leftover chicken or turkey carcass from a Thanksgiving Dinner or a big family dinner. Store the carcass in a freezer bag in the freezer until needed.

Thaw and use within 3 months of freezing.) To make beef stock, replace chicken with 2 pounds of beef bones. Increase the simmering time to 2 hours. Strain the liquid and remove solids.

Refrigerate for 1 hour. Remove the fat layer from the surface and refrigerate until ready to use.

MASTER DOG CHEF CHICKEN SOUP

2 cups Chicken Run stock1/4 cup water
1 raw chicken thigh with bone
1 small clove garlic

(Makes enough for one extra hungry or under-the-weather dog)

Simmer Chicken Run stock. Put raw chicken thigh with bone in a blender, along with water and garlic clove. Process into a paste. Stir paste into simmered soup and allow to cool. Serve. Optional: add 1 finely grated raw carrot to simmering Chicken Run stock, chopped fresh parsley, a handful of pre-cooked pasta or a 1/2 teaspoon of raw honey added after the soup has cooled slightly.

SOFT AS A SPANIEL CREAMY POTATO PARSNIP SOUP

1 cup chicken run stock
1 clove garlic, diced
2 Yukon Gold potatoes, cleaned and diced
1/2 parsnip, peeled and diced
1 teaspoon organic apple cider vinegar
optional: cut up chicken or turkey

(For one medium sized dog, does not have to be a Spaniel!)

Add potatoes, parsnips and chicken run stock in a pot. Bring to a boil, then lower heat until chunks are tender. **DON'T OVERCOOK.** Puree in a blender until smooth as a wet spaniel. Add apple cider vinegar and blend for 30 seconds. Put in your dog's bowl to cool. Once cool, add chicken or turkey (either precooked or raw). Serve with a smile.

A LITTER OF IDEAS TO USE
WITH YOUR LEFTOVER SOUP

(use only homemade soup, no commercial canned soup, please!)

SOUP CREAMSICLE
Puree soup with a 1/2 teaspoon of honey. Transfer the mixture into ice cube trays and freeze. Great for a hot day treat for your dog!

CHOWDER CAKES
Mix soup with bread crumbs (see bread crumb recipe) and 1 to 2 eggs, depending on the soup/bread crumb ratio. Form into cakes and cook in a small toaster oven for 10 minutes at 400 degrees. Serve cool.

CHICKEN RUN POT PIE CASSEROLE
Mix chicken run stock or other soup with small chunks of uncooked chicken and cooked egg noodles. Bake in preheated oven at 400 degrees for 15 minutes and serve cool.

CHOW CHOW BREAD CRUMBS
To make soft bread crumbs, place cut up pieces of firm bread in blender or food processor. Process until no large pieces remain. Do not use white bread, that's as nutritious as a paper towel!

HONEY RECIPES

(Use only **raw, unfiltered honey**. Never heat or cook it!)

HONEY BEE BUTTER
(Makes 2 cups)

1 cup raw, unfiltered honey
1 cup softened (by room temperature) unsalted butter

Mix together until blended. Store covered in refrigerator.

HONEY-GLAZED VEGGIES

2 cups mixed and diced red potatoes, zucchini, carrots and sweet potatoes.
1/4 cup honey/butter mixture

Steam potatoes first until soft as a puppy's tummy. Set aside. Steam veggies for 5 minutes. Put together with potatoes and mix with the honey/mixture. Serve separate or with raw or slightly cooked meat.

HONEY BEE BUTTER-MIXTURE CAN ALSO BE PUT ON:
• bread (not white bread!)
• apples (chopped or cooked, see Apple Yogi)
• carrot sticks
• popcorn
• chicken or turkey meat

HONEY BEE BUTTER PLUS

Another reminder to never cook the honey/butter mixture. Cooked honey turns to sugar in your dog's digestive system. Your dog does not need sugar!

1/2 cup popcorn
1/4 cup honey/butter mixture

POMERANIAN POPCORN BALLS

Pop popcorn (preferably air popped). Put small amounts of popcorn in a bowl and blend with 1 Tablespoon at a time of honey/butter mixture. Form small Pomeranian balls with your hands. Put popcorn balls on a plate and let sit for at least a 1/2 hour to harden. Give as a treat to your dog, even if he's not a Pomeranian! Store extras in a covered container in your refrigerator.

1/2 cup ground muesli
1/2 cup ground turkey
1 small meaty bone
1/2 cup finely chopped veggie (carrots, zucchini or your leftover veggies).
2 cups filtered water

SLOBBER DOG BONE STEW

(Makes enough for 1 slobbering dog) Combine all ingredients and bake covered at 350 degrees for 35 minutes. Cool and serve with a bib! Lots of great stuff can be added to this stew once it's cooked.

Try adding one or more of the following for more added nutrition:
1/4 tsp. lecithin granules
1/2 tsp. kelp powder
1/8 tsp. bone meal powder
a pinch of sea salt
a pinch of rosemary
1/4 tsp. nutritional yeast
1 tsp. flaxseed oil

CHICKEN A LA BORZOI

(Almost enough for 1 Borzoi)

1 cup uncooked
brown rice
1/2 cup chopped carrots
or cucumber
2 1/2 cups filtered water
2 tsp. plain low-fat
yogurt
3 oz. chicken
1 tsp. olive oil

Cook rice in water for 20 minutes. Add chopped chicken and veggies and cook another 25 minutes or until all water is absorbed. Add the yogurt and oil. Stir well. Serve cool.

SCENT HOUND MEATLOAF

2 Tablespoons butter
1 10oz. box of frozen
chopped spinach
1 garlic clove, minced
or 1 cup grated carrots
2 cups fresh bread crumbs
2 pounds ground beef
optional: 1 egg

Blend all ingredients. Shape into a rounded oval and place in ovenproof dish. Bake 30 minutes at 350 degrees. Cool. Serve with rice.

COONHOUND CARROT LOAF

(Makes enough for 1 hyperactive dog or 2 lounging canines)

1 cup grated carrots
1/2 cup ground muesli
1/2 cup cottage cheese
1 Tablespoon butter
1 egg, beaten
2 teaspoons chopped parsley

Place carrots in blender or food processor with remaining ingredients and process until smooth. Pour into buttered loaf pan, and place into a larger pan with water halfway up the sides of the loaf pan. Bake 35 minutes at 350 degrees. Remove to a rack to cool and serve with raw or slightly cooked meat on your best china.

FOR CHUBBY OR SICKLY CANINES TRY THIS:

WAGGIN' TAIL CARROT COCKTAIL

1/4 cup water
1/2 teaspoon organic apple cider vinegar
1 carrot (washed)
1/2 teaspoon olive oil
1 sprig of parsley

Put all ingredients together and blend until the carrot is pulverized. A small amount of raw, organic calves liver can be blended with the mixture for added nutrition. (Your dog may like this enough to lick it up on his own or if he is ill, you can shoot into his mouth with a needle-less syringe).

YOGI'S SHAR PEI PIE

1 cup boiled ground
turkey - strain turkey and
discard water
1/2 cup cottage cheese
1 clove garlic
3 tablespoons grated
carrot
1/4 cup ground muesli
2 eggs

Preheat oven to 375 degrees. In a pie pan, layer the ground turkey, cottage cheese, garlic and grated carrot. In a separate bowl, blend in muesli and eggs. Pour over meat, but do not stir. Bake for 30 minutes. When cool, serve. Store in refrigerator.

TO DROOL FOR LIVER CHIPS

1 pound Liver (beef or
chicken, preferably
organic)
3 cups ground muesli
1/3 cup olive oil
3/4 cup broth from
cooked livers

In a medium sauce pan, boil liver in 2 cups water, reduce to medium high heat and cook for 5 minutes. Remove liver from liquid and set liquid aside. Grind liver in a food processor until it is a fine paste. (About 1 1/2 cups liver paste). Preheat oven to 350 degrees. Combine liver paste and muesli in a large bowl and mix. Add oil and liquid from liver and mix thoroughly. Roll out dough onto lightly floured surface to about a 1/4" thickness. Cut out chips with cookie cutter or bottle cap. Transfer chips to an ungreased baking sheets. Bake for 30 - 35 minutes. Cool chips. Store in an airtight container and refrigerate.

SWEET PUPPY BAKE

(Makes enough for an armload of puppies or 2 grown "puppies")

3 Bananas
1 teaspoon cinnamon
2 Tablespoons lemon juice
3 Tablespoons unsalted butter
2 cups cooked sweet potatoes
2 Tablespoons raw honey

Cut bananas and sprinkle with lemon juice. Blend bananas, sweet potatoes, and cinnamon in food processor until smooth. Spoon into buttered casserole dish. Dot with butter. Bake at 350 degrees for 30 minutes. After casserole is fairly cool, dot with raw honey over the top and serve.

YOUR MOTHER'S A DOG BASIC MUESLI BISCUITS

1 cup ground muesli
1/4 cup olive oil
1 egg
1/4 cup water

Preheat oven to 350 degrees. Combine ground muesli in a large bowl and mix thoroughly with egg, oil and water. Roll dough out onto lightly floured surface to about 1/2 inch thickness. Cut out biscuits with a bone shaped cookie cutter or if you're desperate, use a bottle cap. Transfer biscuits to an ungreased baking sheet. Bake for 15 to 25 minutes for very small biscuits, 30 to 40 minutes for larger biscuits. Cool and store in airtight container in refrigerator.

TO MAKE MORE EXCITING BASIC MUESLI BISCUITS ADD THE FOLLOWING:

Lamb, chicken, turkey, or beef meat. You can use your choice of meat raw or you can boil first in water for 5 minutes. For lamb and beef, separate meat from the bones, then grind very fine in a food processor with a 1/4 to 1/2 cup of water to create a paste. For chicken and turkey, take the meat, including the bones, and individually grind each piece with 1/4 cup of water and create a pate (bones and all). Take this pate and combine with 1 extra cup of ground muesli because of the additional meat pate. You will have to use your common sense and compensate for the wet and dry ingredients on an individual recipe basis.

You can also add to these basic biscuits:
- 1 clove of garlic
- 1/4 cup mashed apples
- add a dollop of honey/butter mixture on top
of each biscuit after cooked.

TERRIER TUNA BISCUITS

1 can (8 oz.) tuna in water, strained.
2 - 3 cups ground muesli (adjust to individual recipe)
1/2 cup water
2/3 cup olive oil

Preheat oven to 350 degrees. Drain water from tuna in can. Combine muesli, tuna, water and oil and mix thoroughly. Roll dough out onto lightly floured surface to about a 1/2 inch thickness. Cut out biscuits with a cookie cutter. Transfer to an ungreased baking sheet. Bake for 15 to 25 minutes for small biscuits or 30 to 35 minutes for larger biscuits. Cool. Store in airtight container and refrigerate.

MUTT FOOD

Mutt Food is not only for mutts, it's for all dogs. It's a combination of ideas of food for your dog. Steamed or slightly cooked leftovers can be used with raw or slightly cooked meat. Please - no overcooked or fried food!

- Raw or slightly boiled Chicken, prepared Oatmeal (or muesli), and Rice
- Raw or slightly boiled Chicken, cooked Pasta and steamed Vegetables
- Raw or slightly boiled Chicken, cooked Rice and steamed Vegetables
- Raw Beef Heart, cooked Pasta, and quality Dry Dog Food
- Raw Beef Heart, cooked Rice, and steamed Vegetables
- Steamed Fish Fillet, cooked Rice, steamed Carrot, and Cottage Cheese
- Raw Ground Beef, cooked Pasta, Hard Cheese, scrambled or soft-boiled Egg, steamed Carrot
- Plain Yogurt, a dab of raw Honey, whole-grain Bread Crumbs, Hard Cheese
- Prepared Oatmeal or Muesli mix, mashed Apple, Hard Cheese

QUICKIES FOR SNACKS OR FAST DAYS

- Cream Cheese with Strawberries
- Plain Yogurt with homemade Dog Biscuits
- Plain Yogurt with boiled Egg and Lettuce Leaves
- Cooked Rice with boiled Vegetables and Cottage Cheese
- Scrambled Egg with grated Hard Cheese, Avocado and cooked Pasta

YOGI'S DREAMLAND BARBEQUE

Share a barbeque with your dog!

Cut chunks of beef or lamb and put on a skewer along with a few chunks of veggies. Grill on the barbecue for no longer then 5 minutes. Put meat and vegetable chunks in your dog's bowl along with a small amount of precooked potatoes. Drizzle raw, honey over all ingredients and serve when cool.

GREAT MUTTER DESSERTS!

APPLE YOGI

1 apple
1 clove garlic
dash of cinnamon
(optional)
1 teaspoon raw, unsalted butter, at room temperature (optional)
or 1/4 cup olive oil
1/2 teaspoon raw honey
(optional)

Wash apple. Cut off tip of apple. Remove a small bit of the center (enough to put a cut up clove of garlic in). Put apple upright in baking dish in center of oven for 10 to 15 minutes at preheated 350 degrees. remove apple and put on stove top to cool. drizzle honey/butter mixture over warm apple. Add cinnamon. Cut apple in several halves, enough for your size dog to eat. Slightly mix all ingredients. Great for a treat once a week. For small dogs, use small apples.

HAPPY CAKE

Double "Your Mother's A Dog Basic Muesli Biscuit" mix, but instead of cutting into biscuits, spread into a buttered cake pan. Cook for 30 to 35 minutes at 350 degrees or until done in center of cake.

Meat pate can also be added to the biscuit mix to make as a cake.

For frosting, add a mixture of whipped cream cheese and honey. Spread on cake. Use carob chips to mark dog's name on the cake.

ANOTHER CAKE CRUST CAN BE MADE FROM A GRAHAM CRACKER CRUST. YOU CAN LOOK IN HEALTH FOOD STORES FOR GRAHAM CRACKERS MADE WITH FRUIT JUICE FOR SWEETENING INSTEAD OF SUGAR.

TO MAKE THE GRAHAM CRACKER CRUST:

1 1/2 cups graham cracker crumbs (put graham crackers in blender to make crumbs).
1/4 cup softened unsalted butter

In a medium bowl, combine graham cracker crumbs and butter. Stir to combine. Press crumb mixture into a 9 inch pan. Chill for 30 minutes. Add filling of whipped cream cheese, meat paste, scrambled eggs, mashed bananas, etc.

RESOURCES

OF COURSE, THERE'S A SOURCE !

FRESH DOG FOOD
Noah's Kingdom Dog Food Pre-Mix
Atlantic Highlands, NJ
800-662-4711

Sojourner Farms
European-Style Pet Food Mix
Minneapolis, MN
888-867-6567 www.sojos.com

Monzie's Organics
Organic Muesli For Dogs
Sebastopol, CA
707-824-1031 www.monzies.com

FERMENTED MEAT
BalanceDiet
Veterinary Nutrition Corporation
Las Cruces, NM
888-777-0505

FREEZE DRIED MEAT
Steve's Real Food for Dogs
Eugene, OR
800-968-1738 www.realdogfood.com
FROZEN, RAW MEAT - READY PREPARED
Grandad's Pet Food
Santa Clara, CA
408-727-6160 www.grandadspetfoods.com

Feed This Pet Food
Forestville, CA
707-887-1122 www.feedthis.com

Pat McKay, Inc.
Pasadena, CA
800-975-7555 www.home1.gte.net/patmckay

Animal Food Services, Inc.
Iola, WI
800-743-0322

Fresh Food Momma
Fair Oaks, CA
916-967-6255 freshmomm@softcom.net

BETTER QUALITY DOG FOOD
Back to Basics
Beowulf Natural Feeds, Inc.
Altmar, NY
800-219-2558 / 315-298-7366

PHD Pet Products, Inc.
White Plains, NY
800-PHD-1502

Regal Pet Food
Lutherville, MD
800-638-7006

Wysong Dog Food
Midland, MI
800-748-0233

California Natural
Natura Pet Products
Santa Clara, CA
800-532-7261 / 408-261-0770

Canidae
Canidae Corp.
San Luis Obispo, CA
800-398-1600 / 805-544-4470

Flint River
Flint River Ranch
Riverside, CA
909-682-5048

Innova
Natura Pet Products
Santa Clara, CA
800-532-7261

Limited Diet (for dogs with food allergies)
Innovative Veterinary diets
Corona, CA
800-359-4483 / 909-278-4280

Pinnacle
Breeder's Choice
Irwindale, CA
800-255-4286 / 626-334-9301

Solid Gold
El Cajon, CA
(west coast) 800-DOG-HUND/ (east coast) 800-521-0010

Spot's Stew (Canned Dog Food)
Palm Harbor, FL
800-426-4256 www.halopets.com

Wow-Bow Distributors (Vegetarian Dog Food)
516-254-6064

Burns Real Food for Dogs (call for free Natural Health Guide)
Joohn Burns MRCVS
Chesterton, IN
877-983-9651 www.bpn4u.com

GREAT NATURAL TREATS
Twisted Biscuit (They give 5% of gross sales to animal charities)
Vancouver, WA
360-885-7815 www.twistedbiscuit.com
Mollywood Squares
www.treatoria.com

Monzie's Organic Cookies for Dogs - Free Catalog
707-824-1031 www.monzies.com (1% of their gross sales goes
    to Animal Rights Organizations)

Rosebud Inc.
Pray, MT
877-ROSEBUD www.rosiesrewards.com

Sojourner Farms
888-867-6567 www.sojos.com

Once Upon A Dog
Quinoa Dog Biscuit
877-389-8300 www.onceuponadog.com

Lucys Barkery
Parkville, MO
816-587-1980 www.lucysbarkery.com

Love Snax
Calistoga, CA
707-942-2188 www.lovesnax.com

California Natural Health Bar
Natura Pet Products
Santa Clara, CA
800-532-7261

Doggie Divines (Chicken Carrot)
Brunzi's Best
Garrison, NY
877-278-6947

Liver Biscotti
Woolf Products
Concord, CA
888-500-3647

Liver Crisps
Dancing Dog Bakery
Creswell, OR
541-895-5950

Burt's Bones
Burt's Bees, Inc.
Raleigh, NC
800-849-7112

Mr. Barky's Vegetarian Dog Biscuits
Pet Guard
Orange Park, FL
800-874-3221

Poochie Pretzels
Molly's Gourmutt Bakery
Poway, CA
887-468-6888

Cluckers (Chicken Treats for Dogs)
800-759-9439 www.hillbillysmokehouse.com

Plaid Dog Turkey Tenders Treats
St. Paul Pet
651-260-7132 www.stpaulpet.com

Thunder Paws Treats (call for catalog)
Lebanon, PA
717-272-9977

Tia Chips (Wheat & Sugar Free Treats)
877-633-4800 www.tiapetfoods.com

OLIVE OIL
St. Helena Olive Oil Co.
St.Helena, CA
800-939-9880 www.sholiveoil.com

NATURAL RAWHIDE CHEWS AND BONES
Drs. Foster and Smith Super Deluxe Rawhide Chews, "Natural Flavor," or Super Heavyweight Bones
800-826-7206
New England Serum Co. Premium Natural Rawhide Bones
800-637-3786

Pet Factory American Beef-Hide Chews
800-468-3315

Ecology Rawhide Treats
800-709-1567

NATURAL SUPPLEMENTS AND PRODUCTS
NUPRO (liver flavored gravy with supplements)
Nutri-Pet Research, Inc.
New Jersey
800-360-3300 www.nuprosupplements.com

Fresh Factors
Springtime, Inc.
Cockeysville, MD
800-521-3212 / 410-771-8430

Prozyme Products, LTD. (Probiotics)
Lincolnwood, IL
800-522-5537

Missing Link (Super Pet Food Supplement)
Designing Health, Inc.
Valencia, CA
800-774-7387 www.designinghealth.com

Wysong Institute
Midland MI
800-748-0188 www.wysong.net

Merritt Naturals
888-463-7748 www.merrittnaturals.com

FloraZyme (digestive enzyme)
Pet's Friend, Inc.
954-720-0794

"Shake N Zyme" (Digestive enzyme/ Probiotic)
Dancing Paws
Pacific Palisades, CA
888-644-PAWS

Willard Water
Nutrition Coalition
Fargo, ND
800-447-4793 www.willardswater.com

North Star Natural Pet Products
Tinmouth, VT
802-446-2812

Pet Therapy (Chinese Medicine for Pets)
A Path to Wellness
800-658-2225

Wow-Bow Distributors -Free Catalog
516-254-6064

Nature's Path (Pet-Lyte Liquid Electrolytes)
941-426-3375

Seaweeds and Micronutrients for animals
Source, Inc.
Branford, CT
800-232-2365

Spirulina for Pets (Blue-green algae)
Earthuse Animal Health
Tollhouse, CA
800-995-0681

Homeopathic Medicines and Nutritional Supplements
Dr. Goodpet
Inglewood, CA
800-222-9932

Chinese Herbal Formulas
Herb-cetera
New Britain, CT
860-826-8725

Bighorn Botanicals (Natural teas, tinctures and salves for dogs)
Noxon, MT
406-847-5597

Complete Line of Holistic Products
Dynamite Specialty Products
Meridian, ID
800-677-0919

Nutritional Supplements and Neutraceutical Formulas
Pet Power Inc. (Products from the beehive)
Phoenix, AZ
800-875-0096

Canine Medicine Chest (Good website help for sick dogs)
712-644-3535 www.caninemedicinechest.com

Prime Of Life (Chewable Supplement Tablets)
From Best Friends Animal Sanctuary
800-864-1661 www.bestfriends.org

NATURAL FLEA CONTROL
Hop Off (Nutritional Supplement)
Marston Mills, MA
800-393-6666 www.hopoff.com

Fleas Flee (Nutritional Supplement)
Chestnut Ridge, NY
914-356-3838
GROW YOUR OWN FOOD
Territorial Seed Company
Cottage Grove, OR
888-657-3131 www.territorialseed.com

Gardener's Supply Co.
800-427-3363 www.gardeners.com

Gardens Alive (Includes natural care products and supplements
   for pets)
Lawrenceburg, IN
812-537-8650

EarthBox (Great for apartment dwellers or anyone short of out
   door space
for a home garden. Now there's no excuse!)
St. Petersburg, FL
800-750-1066

MAIL ORDER CATALOGS
Chamisa Ridge (A catalog with herbs, books, toys and treats for
    dogs)
Santa Fe, NM
800-743-3188 www.chamisaridge.com

The Vitamin Shoppe (Vitamins & Minerals for pets and people)
800-223-1216 www.VitaminShoppe.com

Pet Sage (Pet care catalog)
Alexandria, VA
800-738-4584 www.petsage.com

Whiskers (Chemical free pet products)
New York, NY
800-944-7537 Free catalog
In The Company Of Dogs
Portland, TN
800-924-5050

Allpets
800-346-0749 www.allpets.com

Pet Warehouse
800-443-1160 www.petwhse.com

Doctors Foster & Smith
800-826-7206 www.DrsFosterSmith.com

Home Pet Shop
800-346-0749 www.PetQuarters.com

MAGAZINES/NEWSLETTERS ABOUT DOGS
The Bark
Berkeley, CA
www.thebark.com

The Whole Dog Journal
Palm Coast, FL
800-829-9165

Bonkers!
Palm Beach, FL
800-777-1999 www.goingbonkers.com

JOURNALS FOR YOUR DOG'S LIFE
Pet Health Journal
530-342-1380 www.PetHealthJournal.com

TRAVELING WITH YOUR DOG
Iceless Coolers (Portable Coleman Thermal Electric Cooler with adapters for AC power and for 12 volt battery adapting to your cigarette lighters, etc.)
Auto Sport
Charlottesville,VA
800-726-1199

Handi-Drink Hiking Water Bottle with drinking bowl
Macke International
Malibu, CA
877-241-5300

The Outward Hound Traveling Bottle and Bowl
The Kyjen Company
800-477-5735 www.kyjen.com

Silver Pet Supplies (Pet Travel bags, Day Hike Fanny Packs, Dog Backpacks and Pet Gear Bags)
877-738-8691 www.Silverpet.com

Redbarn Dog Food (Compressed meat loaf)
800-775-3849 www.redbarninc.com

Eileen's Directory of Pet Friendly Lodging
800-638-3637

Pets Welcome
Bon Vivant Press
Monterey, CA
Fax: 408-373-3567

Vacationing With Your Pet
by Eileen Barish
800-496-2665

Also:
www.takeyourpet.com
www.aaa.com

COOKING/ BAKING EQUIPMENT
Natural Lifestyle Mail Order Market (Our Absolute Favorite for
   everything from pots and pans to natural food!)
Asheville, NC
800-752-2775 www.natural-lifestyle.com

Dean & Deluca
New York
800-221-7714

Williams-Sonoma
San Francisco, CA
800-541-2233

The Kitchen Witch
Encinitas, CA
619-942-3228

Chefs
Dallas, TX
800-967-3291 www.chefscatalog.com

Albert Uster Imports, Inc.
Gaithersburg, MD
800-231-8154

Vita-Mix (Super Blender/ Processor)
800-848-2649 www.vitamix.com

MEAT SAFETY QUESTIONS
United States Department of Agriculture, Food Safety Department
Consumer questions - 10am to 4pm, EST
800-535-4555

U.S. Department of Agriculture Web Site
ams.usda.gov/farmersmarkets/map.htm

National Farmers' Market Directory
Box 96456
Washington, DC 20090
202-720-8317

Meat & Poultry Hotline
800-535-4555

Animal Poison Hotline
888-232-8870

CHICKEN RANCH MEAT
Shelton's (free range chicken)
Pomona, CA
909-623-4361

ALTERNATIVE SOURCES OF FAMILY FARM MEAT & POULTRY
List of Alternative Suppliers
www.factoryfarm.org/alternativeproducers.html

More Information on our Food System
Food First
www.foodfirst.org

For Corporate Takeovers in the Food Industry
home.earthlink.net/~avkrebs/CARP/#anchor1

Family Farm Crisis
www.farmcrisis.net
www.cfra.org

Organizations Concerned with Factory Farming
United Poultry Concerns
www.upc-online.org

Families Against Rural Messes
www.farmweb.org
www.sierraclub.org/cafos
www.worc.org
www.caff.org

How to choose a Humane Diet
www.hsus.org/programs/farm/diet/index.html

VETERINARY NUTRITION CONSULTANT
Russell Swift, DVM
Tamarac, FL
561-391-5615

PET NUTRITION CONSULTANTS
Celeste Yarnall
Beverly Hills, CA
888-235-7387 - 310-278-1385

Pat McKay, Inc.
Pasadena, CA
order line - 800-975-7555 or 626-296-1120

HOLISTIC VETERINARIANS
American Holistic Veterinary Medical Association
www.altvetmed.com

Veterinary Institute for Therapeutic Alternatives
Sherman, CT
860-354-2287

Academy of Veterinary Homeopathy
305-652-1590
www.acadvethom.org

NATURAL CARE FOR PETS
Canine Medicine Chest - (a great site for information on using natural healing products, including products for sale)
www.caninemedicinechest.com

PET AND PEOPLE SUPPORT SERVICES
PAWS - Pets Are Wonderful Support - (services to help people care for their companion animals while dealing with life threaten ing illnesses)
San Francisco, CA
415-241-1460
Los Angeles, CA
322-876-PAWS

CHARITY WATCHDOG SERVICES
Where to look up a non-profit online for a gander at where and how they spend your donations
www.tess.org
www.guidestar.org

BOOKS
ANIMALS AS TEACHERS & HEALERS Susan Chemack McElroy
ANIMAL NUTRITION John D. Rowe
ANIMALS...OUR RETURN TO WHOLENESS Penelope Smith
ARE YOU POISONING YOUR PET? Nina Anderson & Howard Peiper
BACK TO BASICS Wendy Volhard
BONE APPETIT COOKBOOK Anson
CHOOSING THE BEST FOOD FOR YOUR BREED OF DOG William D. Cusick
CONSUMER'S GUIDE TO DOG FOOD: WHAT'S IN DOG FOOD, WHY IT'S THERE, AND HOW TO CHOOSE THE BEST FOOD FOR YOUR DOG Liz Palika
DR. PITCAIRN'S COMPLETE GUIDE TO NATURAL HEALTH FOR

DOGS AND CATS Dr. Richard Pitcairn & Susan Hubble Pitcairn
EARL MINDELL NUTRITION & HEALTH FOR DOGS Earl Mindell & Elizabeth Renaghan
FEED YOUR PUP WITH BONES Ian Billinghurst
FEEDING STRATEGY (SURVIVAL IN THE WILD) Jennifer Owen
FOOD PETS DIE FOR Ann Martin
FOUR PAWS, FIVE DIRECTIONS: A GUIDE TO CHINESE MEDICINE FOR CATS AND DOGS Cheryl Schwartz
GIVE YOUR DOG A BONE Ian Billinghurst
HEAL YOUR DOG THE NATURAL WAY Richard Allport, B.Vet.Med
HOW TO HAVE A HEALTHIER DOG Wendell O. Belfield, DVM & Martin Zucker
INVESTIGATIVE REPORT ON PET FOOD Animal Protection Institute of America
IT'S FOR THE ANIMALS! COOKBOOK Helen L. McKinnon
KINSHIP WITH ALL LIFE Allen J. Boone
NATURAL CARE OF PETS Donald I. Ogden, DVM
NATURAL DOG CARE Celeste Yarnall
NATURAL HEALING FOR DOGS AND CATS Diane Stein
NATURAL INSECT REPELLENTS Janette Grainger & Connie Moore
NATURAL FOOD RECIPES FOR HEALTHY DOGS Carol Boyle
NATURAL REARING DIRECTORY An annual directory of breeders who feed raw foods www.naturalrearing.com
NATURAL REMEDIES FOR DOGS & CATS CJ Puotinen
NO BARKING AT THE TABLE COOKBOOK: MORE RECIPES YOUR DOG WILL BEG FOR Wendy Nan Rees
REIGNING CATS & DOGS Pat McKay
THE COMPLETE HERBAL HANDBOOK FOR THE DOG & CAT Juliette de Bairacli Levy
THE ENCYCLOPEDIA OF NATURAL PET CARE CJ Puotinen
THE HEALING TOUCH Dr. Michael Fox, MRCVS
THE HOLISTIC GUIDE FOR A HEALTHY DOG Wendy Volhard & Kerry Brown, DVM
THE NATURAL DOG Mary L. Brennan, DVM
THE ORIGINAL GOURMET DOGGIE TREAT COOKBOOK Carole Laybourn

THE TRADITIONAL FLOWER REMEDIES OF DR. EDWARD BACH Leslie J. Kaslof
THE ULTIMATE DIET: NATURAL NUTRITION FOR DOGS & CATS Kymythy R. Schultze
THE WOLF WITHIN: A NEW APPROACH TO CARING FOR YOUR DOG David Alderton

DOG BOOK ORDERING
Besides ordering the above books from your local bookstore or amazon.com, they can be ordered from:
Dogwise - 800-776-2665 www.dogwise.com
Dog Lovers Bookshop - 212-369-7554 www.dogbooks.com

What are you waiting for? Start ordering, get cooking!!!

WE ASSUME...

Yogi and I assume a lot in this book. We also assume that you know when to take your dog to your veterinarian to rule out any major complications or disease before creating a new diet for him. We also assume that you and your vet will work together and learn new ideas from each other about your dog.

Any ideas or recipes in this book should be given to your dog slowly and in small increments. It is impossible to write a book and generalize for every dog and how they will react. You are ultimately responsibile for the health of your dog. We have assumed that you know that.

DOG CHEFS OF AMERICA™ PRODUCTS

10% of our profits goes to feed stray and
homeless dogs or to support spay and neuter programs!
Go to www.dogchefs.com to order our products or use
the order form on the next page.
If you think you have qualified for a COMMON SENSE
DEGREE after reading this book, fill out the order form,
including $3 for shipping, and we will proudly send you
one to be displayed on your wall.
To order any of the above, contact us or send in the
order form to:
Dog Chefs of America™
PO Box 1099
Calistoga, CA 94515
888-322-8099 (toll free)
Email: dogchefs@napanet.net
www.dogchefs.com

ABOUT AUTHORS

Micki Voisard gives cooking classes and seminars on home prepared meals and road food creations for dogs. She has been speaking
on health for dogs for 10 years and is an author, artist and radio talk
show host. She and her husband, David, live with two dogs and six
cats in Northern California.

Yogi Voisard is a rescued Chinese Shar Pei and test markets all of
Micki's creations. He is aware of being "one lucky dog."

YOGI

MICKI

order form

Send orders to: Dog Chefs of America
POB 1099, Calistoga, CA 94515 — or order online at: www.dogchefs.com
You can also contact us at: 888-322-8099 E-mail: dog chefs@napanet.net

the book

Becoming the Chef Your Dog Thinks You Are: the book your dog has been drooling for! $14.95

the t-shirt

A white cotton t-shirt silkscreened in black, proudly tells the world:
"I'm becoming the person my dog thinks I am!" along with a "Happy Dog" logo (on back),
while the front sports the "Happy Dog" logo. Sizes: Medium, Large, Extra Large. $16.

the HAT

100% cotton, washed twill, 6-panel cap. One size fits all. Choose "Happy Dog" or "Stray Dog" logo.
Colors: Mocha with Navy brim or Stone with Black brim. $16.

the APRON

Embroidered in black, on a white, full-length apron with pockets is the "Happy Dog" logo and:
"I'm becoming the chef my dog thinks I am!" $22.

COMMON SENSE degree

I qualify for a "Common Sense Degree"! $3.

| Quantity | Item | Color | Size | Logo choice (below) for hats only | | Price | Total |
				HappyDog	StrayDog		

METHOD OF PAYMENT

............Check/Money Order............Master Card............Visa

Credit Card #..

Exp. Date (MM/YY)..

Signature...

SHIPPING CHARGES
$4.95 for first item
$1.00 for each add'l item

Sub Total	
CA Residents 7.50% Sales Tax	
Shipping Charges (See Left)	
Total	

FOR HATS ONLY: Choose a logo for each hat ordered

← OR →

SOLD TO: (please print)

Name...

Address..

City...State...........Zip...............

Telephone (.............)...